YOU'RE IN BUSINESS!
BUILDING BUSINESS ENGLISH SKILLS

JOHN THOMAS FRENCH
Northrop University Language Institute

▲▼ **Addison-Wesley Publishing Company**

Additional material: 1 cassette recording C-90 of readings (ISBN 0-201-11499-2)

Photographs from: pp. 2 and 118, Santa Fe Railway Photographs; p. 18, courtesy of New York Stock Exchange; p. 34, courtesy of Apple Computer Inc.; p. 48, Boeing Photo; p. 66, courtesy of BASF Wyandotte Corporation; pp. 73–77, courtesy of Northrop University; p. 86, courtesy of Mack Trucks, Inc.; p. 100, courtesy of Dow Jones & Company, Inc.; p. 120, reprinted with permission from the Los Angeles Times; p. 138, Ellis Herwig/Stock Boston; pp. 144–5, courtesy of Harris Lumber Company; p. 160, courtesy of the Coca-Cola Company; p. 178, courtesy of NCR Corporation.

ISBN 0-201-11498-4

22 23 24 25 CRS 02 01 00

Preface

This book was written to meet the needs of the foreign student who is intending to study business at an American university. It is also suitable for students of English anywhere whose primary reason in learning English is for the purpose of conducting business. Many business professionals who need to conduct negotiations in English will find this book useful for learning business terminology and concepts. This book is written so that it can be used by an individual studying on his own or by an instructor as a classroom textbook.

The topics which were selected for this text deal with basic areas of business. The topics are common to many introductory textbooks on business, and therefore, a student who has completed this text will have an introduction to some of the material he will study later along with an understanding of the terminology of the field. There is a variety of topics which should be of interest to the businessman who is involved in international trade, negotiations, or financing. The topics are presented in an order paralleling the development of a business from a sole proprietorship to a multinational corporation. Each lesson is introduced and related to the previous material.

This text emphasizes several skills which both the student and professional need to develop if they are to conduct business in English. First, there are several types of vocabulary exercises. Emphasis is placed on developing the ability to learn meanings from context. Next, there is listening practice which prepares the student and professional to be able to listen to others and make notes about the important points. This is an important skill for the student who attends lectures and for the professional who must be able to listen to discussions and presentations and take part in negotiations. Reading exercises teach the student to grasp what a writer has said by analyzing the passage to find the main ideas, to note details, and to make inferences. Writing exercises are included in order to help the student develop and express his own thoughts or opinion about a topic related to the lesson. Emphasis is placed on developing different methods of approaching problems, such as analysis, contrast, analogy, etc. Developing these skills will benefit the user of the book, no matter what type of business decisions he is called upon to make. There are also proposals for debates at the end of each lesson to enable the student to use orally some of the words and ideas that have been learned in the course of the unit.

The variety and scope of the exercises, together with the information given in the reading selections, should further develop both English language skills and student comprehension of the basic elements of business. This book not only provides a good foundation for continuing a more specialized study in the field, it also illustrates techniques that will be useful to the professional in understanding and writing up presentations in the world of business.

Contents

2 Legal Forms of Organization   17

3 Production   33

6 Marketing   85

7 Distribution   99

8 Promotion   117

9 Financial Statements   137

10 International Business   159

11 Computers 177

Using the Text

To the Instructor

The purpose of this text is to acquaint the non-English speaker who already has some background in the English language with the terms used in modern business English. The topics of the chapters are general to all types of business, and they are explained and defined in such a way that a teacher need not have a business background in order to use this text.

Each unit consists of a written text, several types of exercises: vocabulary exercises, reading comprehension exercises, listening and note-taking exercises, and a vocabulary review. There is also a writing assignment and a topic for discussion or debate.

The teacher may find it convenient to record the text on tape. This should be done at normal reading speed and at a slower deliberate speed. The tape can be played as the students follow along with the text, and the slower speed can be used for developing note-taking skills and pronunciation practice.

Depending on the level of the class, it may be possible to play the normal speed tape as an introduction to the material. The advantage of playing the tape is that it forces the student to consider the entire text quickly without becoming bogged down by the individual words. This is good practice for listening to a conversation or a lecture.

Before reading the text, the students should look over the glossary at the end of each lesson and become familiar with the difficult vocabulary used in that lesson. In general, the vocabulary building exercises should be done immediately after reading the text. The words glossed in the margin of the reading selections are simplified clarifications of the word or phrase underlined in the text. They are not intended as exact synonyms or substitutions for the more difficult expression. The text should be read several times during the course of each lesson until the student is familiar with all the words and expressions. It can be read silently or played on a tape recorder, so that eventually the students can read it fluently.

The listening and note-taking exercises are to be done after an initial reading of the text. There is a short explanation to the student at the beginning of this section. The student should be familiar with the vocabulary at this point. These exercises, too, can be read (or played from a recording) section by section to the class at a deliberate speed. The purpose of these exercises is to teach the student to grasp ideas and to see the relationship between them. It is suggested that the instructor have the students work one exercise followed by discussion before going on to the next exercise.

The vocabulary review forces the student to look at the text one more time and to read it through in totality after having learned the meanings of the words.

The last exercise involves writing a paragraph. The instructor should review the basics of good sentence structure and grammar as required, depending upon the ability of the students. Since this is not an elementary text, it is expected that students will already be able to write sentences about the topic without copying word-for-word from the text. The goal here is to use the vocabulary of the lesson correctly as well as to present a topic in a clear and logical order. Individual conferences with students to assist with revisions of the paragraphs are quite helpful if time allows.

The debates are supplementary exercises which can be used to help students acquire the new concepts and ideas as active vocabulary, as well as to foster their skills in logical organization and oral argumentation. If possible, representatives from the business world could be brought in as guests to discuss these topics with the class. The debates should be assigned in advance so that the students can both prepare their own arguments and be familiar with those of the opposing side. For a more interesting debate, the group should be divided in half, with some of the stronger and weaker students on each side. A representative from each side should be designated to present the opening statement, and another to summarize the arguments presented. If the group is very large, a five-minute time limit can be set for the individual arguments and answers. This will help to avoid repetition and encourage clear, logical, and concise statements.

To the Student

This book will help you learn business words and concepts. You should begin each lesson by looking at the glossary with the vocabulary exercises. They will help you learn the meanings of the words. If you see a word you do not know in the reading, you should continue reading until the end of the sentence. Then read the sentence again and try to guess the meaning of the word. If you still have difficulty, read the paragraph completely through, and if necessary, reread the paragraph to try to learn the meanings of the unfamiliar words. You should think about the main idea of the paragraph—what the paragraph is mostly about. You should then be able to guess the meaning of the word. If you cannot guess the meaning, look again at the glossary at the end of the lesson. Try to understand the explanation of the word. After having learned these strategies, if you are still unable to understand the word, you may use your dictionary. But remember: you may need to do the exercises and read the lessons several times before you understand them completely.

Many of the exercises concentrate on a specific section of the text. The note-taking and listening comprehension exercises will teach you how to outline material you read, which is a good way to help you remember it. You learn to recognize details, main ideas, and methods of explaining. You can use the outlines for reviewing the material. To answer the questions in the reading comprehension exercises you need to note details and make inferences. Details are specific items of information and inferences are ideas which occur to you after thinking about what you have read. The details will be found in the text, but the exact answer for an inference question may not be found there. To find it, you need to think about the topic and form your own opinion.

The writing exercise requires you to consider the entire text you have read and how it was written. In order to do the writing exercise, you need to be able to organize all that you have read in a logical order according to the prescribed formula. Writing helps you to determine what your own ideas are and to express them so that others may read them. When you write, you are trying to convince the reader that your ideas and opinions are correct.

Introduction to Lesson One:
Basic Factors in Business

Lesson One discusses the basic factors necessary for any business undertaking. Definitions of business factors are presented by means of examples and explanations. Texts often begin with definitions of the topic and an explanation of why it is worthy of study. Here, the concepts of land, labor, capital, and entrepreneurship are defined and explained as they relate to the field of business.

The text defines the nature of business activity as a necessary social institution and gives an explanation of the role of land, labor, and capital in business. It is the combination of these factors, or entrepreneurship, that enables business to operate. Each factor is discussed by means of examples and operations. The reader should keep the overall organization of the written text in mind. By realizing that each paragraph deals with a particular topic, the reader develops an analytical approach to reading. This approach increases comprehension.

Linguistic concepts important for this lesson are: sentence adverbs, connectors/transition elements, predicate nominatives, and synonyms.

Machines perform the hard physical labor which in earlier times required several workers.

Basic Factors in Business

The Nature of Business

Paragraph 1

Business is the human activity related to material things. It is necessary for civilization. It is found in all societies, even the simplest ones. Business may include the production of goods: making airplanes, building buildings, and constructing paper boxes are examples of production. It can also provide the financing for these activities. Lending money, trading stocks and bonds, and selling insurance policies relate to the <u>securing of capital</u> for business activities. Other forms of business include merchandising, which is the selling of products, and providing various services, such as accounting, distributing, and repair. Business, then, is the activity of producing and distributing goods and services.

getting money

Paragraph 2

In our study of business, it is necessary to understand the four basic factors of production. These four factors are land, labor, capital, and entrepreneurship. What is meant by these four terms?

Paragraph 3

In order to produce things, it is necessary to use land. Here, the term
land is used in the most general way. It refers not only to a piece of real
estate where we might build a factory, but it also means all the raw
materials used for production. Some of these raw materials are found on
give   the earth's surface, such as trees, which <u>yield</u> wood for lumber. Other
raw materials are found under the earth's surface in mines and oil wells,
taken   and still other raw materials may be <u>extracted</u> from the air. All the raw
materials for production come from the land, the air, and the oceans.

Paragraph 4

Labor refers to the use of mental or physical work to produce goods.
Most labor changes raw materials into finished products and then
distributes these to buyers. In industrialized countries, labor is generally
more mental than physical. For example, in both manufacturing and
agriculture, machines accomplish the very tiring physical work that
unskilled laborers used to do. In other industries computer programmed
robots and other forms of data processing equipment perform many of
the jobs which used to require a lot of mental labor. Therefore, to a
certain extent the next factor, capital, can be used to replace labor or
reduce the amount of physical and mental labor that humans have to
do   use in order to <u>conduct</u> business.

Paragraph 5

In everyday language, capital means several things. The most general
meaning is wealth or money. But it also refers to the equipment that
money purchases. As one of the basic factors of production, capital is all
of the things that workers use in production and distribution. It includes their tools, machines, and buildings such as factories and warehouses where goods are produced and stored. Capital, therefore, refers to
anything which helps to produce and distribute goods.

Paragraph 6

Putting together land, labor, and capital to make something of value, is
called entrepreneurship. The entrepreneur is the person responsible for
controlling and directing the other three factors. The entrepreneur does
not make things with his own hands unless he is also a worker. In a
business the workers take orders from the entrepreneur. He is the leader,
and the employees follow his direction.

Paragraph 7

beginning

have new ideas

takes all the chances

Entrepreneurship includes some other important activities. The entrepreneur is responsible for <u>initiating</u> business activity. He must begin his
business by bringing together the land, labor, and capital. Next, he must
manage the business by deciding the general policies for business operation. In order to be successful, an entrepreneur must also <u>be innovative</u>.
He must look for new products or new ways of making things, and new
methods of distribution, or he must offer new services. He must be able
to decide on the value of things which other people invent, whether it is
a new toy, a new method of filing, or a new way of advertising. Finally,
he <u>bears all the risks</u> of the business.

Paragraph 8

people the business
owes money to

activity

Everyone connected with a business shares in the risks of the business.
When a company goes bankrupt, that is, becomes unable to pay its
debts, it causes problems for many people. It is hard for the employees
who may have to seek work elsewhere; the customers must look for
another place to buy their products; <u>creditors</u> usually lose some of the
money that they have lent to the company. But the entrepreneur takes
the biggest risk. If the business succeeds or fails, he must pay them up to
the limit of his ability to pay. If he is skillful—and lucky—the money he
receives from his business <u>venture</u> will pay for the land, labor, and
capital, and there will still be some extra money remaining for him.
This extra money is the profit. If the money he receives from the
business venture is not enough to pay for all of the costs, the difference is
a loss.

Vocabulary Building Introduction

One method of learning new vocabulary while developing reading skills
is to use the context. Many times the context, the sentence or passage in
which the word occurs, will explain the meaning of the word. One way
to spot items defined by context is to look for words which are synonyms
for the verb *to be*. Examples are *such as, refers to, consists of, involves,
includes, means.*

A: Vocabulary in context

show

Paragraph 1 is a text which gives definitions and examples. After you
have read Paragraph 1, write down the expressions that <u>indicate</u> definitions, examples, and explanations.

EXAMPLE   Business *is* the human activity related to material things.

Besides words that indicate definitions, there are other techniques of using context to arrive at a meaning. Sometimes the verb in the sentence will explain what the function of the subject is, for example: A *creditor* lends money which usually is paid back in a certain time with interest. Similarly, the object or another element of the sentence may suggest the meaning of a word.

Study the sentences below in which the underlined words are explained by the context.

1. Business is the activity of making and distributing goods and services.
2. Land refers to the sources of raw materials needed for production.
3. Labor is the use of mental or physical work to produce goods.
4. Capital means not only wealth, but all the things that workers use in production and distribution which are purchased with money.
5. Entrepreneurship is the activity of controlling and directing the other three factors.
6. The money that he makes is the profit.
7. If the money he receives is not enough to pay for all the costs, the difference is a loss.
8. When a company goes bankrupt, it is unable to pay its debts.
9. An innovative company is one which continues to provide new goods and services.
10. The entrepreneur initiates business activity by bringing together land, labor, and capital to begin a new business venture.

B: Matching

Match the words below with the definition indicated by the sentences above. Write the number of the word on the line before the definition.

1. initiate	_15_	a . something which must be paid
2. profit	_5_	b . having new products and ideas
3. labor	_1_	c . begin new business activity
4. business	_6_	d . person who directs the business
5. innovative	_7_	e . land
6. entrepreneur	_3_	f . what workers provide

7. raw materials	_8_	g . a business activity
8. venture	_2_	h . money the entrepreneur receives
9. loss	_10_	i . money which buys machines and tools
10. capital	_11_	j . products
11. goods	_12_	k . things which business provides in addition to goods
12. services	_13_	l . describes a company with not enough money and too many debts
13. bankrupt	_9_	m. the result of expenses being more than sales
14. company	_4_	n . the activity of producing goods
15. debt	_14_	o . a business

C: Completion

This exercise is designed to increase vocabulary and reading comprehension. Select the answer which best completes the meaning of the sentence.

1. Advertising is a kind of public announcement which describes the benefits of using a product or service. We can use advertising to increase the sales of our product or service. We expect to find advertising

   a. at school.　　　c. on the land.
   b. in the factory.　(d.) on TV and radio.

2. There is an expression, "It takes money to make money." We know that capital can be used to make something of value. Therefore, capital can refer to

   a. a basic factor.　c. raw materials.
   (b.) money.　　　d. bankruptcy.

3. A creditor is a person to whom the business owes money. Which of the following is most likely to be a creditor?

   a. an entrepreneur.　(c.) a banker.
   b. an employee.　　d. a factor.

4. Labor changes raw materials into finished goods. Paper is an example of a finished good. The raw material would be

   a. physical work.　c. finished products.
   (b.) wood.　　　d. land.

5. Distribution means getting the products from the factory to the store where customers buy them. Which of the following companies would probably be involved in distribution?

   a. a bank.
   b. a transportation company.
   c. a supermarket.
   d. a factory.

6. An employee is a person who works for a company and receives payment for his work. Which factor does the employee supply?

   a. land.
   b. labor.
   c. capital.
   d. innovation.

7. Large companies require more capital than a single entrepreneur could supply. The ownership of the company is therefore divided into shares of stock. In order to raise capital, a company might

   a. risk its future.
   b. bring together land and labor.
   c. sell stock.
   d. produce goods.

8. Value is the quality that makes a thing wanted or worth having. Value is probably

   a. skill.
   b. capital.
   c. price.
   d. profit.

9. Businesses provide both goods and services. Examples of goods are physical products which customers purchase to take home. An example of a service business would be

   a. an oil company.
   b. a store.
   c. a bank.
   d. a factory.

10. The owner of a business takes a risk. He hopes that his business will be successful and that he will make a profit, but there is a chance that he may

   a. manage and direct activities.
   b. offer new services and products.
   c. make a profit.
   d. suffer a loss.

Listening and Note-Taking Skills

The purpose of listening is not only to hear the words, but also to be able to remember what you have heard and to make notes on the most important points. While listening to the entire passage, you must learn to select key words and write them down before the next important point is made. In order to do this you must first learn to notice the overall organization of the material. Good speakers and writers present their ideas in a logical manner. Finding the pattern of organization is the first step in learning how to take notes.

The first paragraph of this lesson is a definition. It explains what business is and gives several examples. It concludes with a summary or restatement of the definition.

There are some words and phrases which might indicate the organization of a passage. For example, when the author says that there are four basic factors in business, you might expect that he will mention the four items and explain something about each one. The passage will most likely be organized in four sections. Certain other phrases like *in summary* or *in conclusion* might show that the statement that follows is the end of a particular part of the discussion.

Here are some important words and phrases which can help you determine the organization of a passage.

Words which indicate the *beginning* of separate sections or points:
ordinal numbers — first, second, etc.
another, one other
besides
further, furthermore
in addition

Words which show the *end* of separate sections:
in conclusion
then
therefore
as a result
finally
lastly
in summary

D: Noting details

The second skill required for good listening is the ability to notice factual details. A detail can be a specific example, a date or other number, or a name. Listen to Paragraph 1 and write down the details in the order in which they are presented in the passage. (The headings can be: examples of production, examples of financing, and examples of services.)

E: Outlining

A technique which you can use for note taking, reading, or writing is outlining. An outline shows the organization of a speaker's or writer's ideas. When you find the pattern of organization, you can make notes in an outline form. Use the writer's cue words to detect the form. The form of your outline will be the same as the organization of the text. What you write in the outline are the factual details.

A system of Roman numerals, letters, and Arabic numerals is used to show the organization of the ideas. The most general ideas are written to the left using Roman numerals. The subheads are indicated by alternating letters and numbers which show the relationship of examples, details, or other important facts to each other. Look at the outline below for Paragraph 1.

I. Definition of Business: activity related to material things needed for civilization

    A. Production
        1. making airplanes
        2. building buildings
        3. constructing paper boxes

    B. Finance
        1. lending money
        2. trading stocks and bonds
        3. selling insurance policies

    C. Other
        1. sales
        2. service
            a. accounting
            b. distributing
            c. repair

Now listen to Paragraphs 2, 3, 4, 5, and 6. (The paragraphs may be repeated as necessary.) Organize your notes into an outline, and fill in the details in the order in which you hear them. Remember the importance of the details is indicated by their position on the outline chart. Begin with: II. Four Factors of Business.

Reading Comprehension

Good writers lead the reader along so that the reader will be convinced by their logical presentation. A good reader should think about what is coming next. He should be able to <u>anticipate</u> the information which a writer will present in his next sentence. If the reader is prepared for what

guess

the writer is about to say, then it will be easier for the reader to pay attention to the passage and remember what he has read. As in listening, certain words serve to indicate what is coming next. For example, if the **includes** first sentence in a paragraph says, "Entrepreneurship <u>involves</u> several important activities . . . ," you should expect that the author will explain what those activities are in the next sentences.

F: Comprehension questions

Read the following questions and think about them as you read Paragraph 7. Try to anticipate what the author is about to say. Then answer the questions about entrepreneurship.

1. How does the entrepreneur initiate business?
2. How does he manage the business?
3. How many activities of entrepreneurship does the author mention?
4. What did you expect Paragraph 8 to explain?

G: Anticipating information

Anticipate what you would expect to find following these sentences and list this information after each one.

1. When a company goes bankrupt, it causes problems for many people.
2. But the entrepreneur takes the biggest risk of all.
3. If he is skillful and lucky, he will make a good profit.

Vocabulary Review: Rephrasing

Rewrite the following sentences. Replace the words *in italics* with expressions from the text which have the same meaning.

H: Rephrasing expressions

1. Everyone connected with a business *takes a chance.*
2. When a company *defaults on its debts*, it causes problems for many people.
3. *Workers* may have to seek *employment* elsewhere.
4. The *owner of the business* takes the greatest risk.
5. *People to whom the company owes money* may lose.

Writing

I: Writing a paragraph

Write a paragraph about the four basic factors of business. Your first sentence should be a topic sentence. It should state what the four basic factors are. Then you should write two sentences about each of the factors. You should discuss the factors in the same order in which they were presented in the lesson. However, do not copy exactly from the lesson.

Oral Practice

Debate

Resolved: Business being essential for all economies, any society that does not put the needs of business first cannot be successful. (Present the arguments for and against this statement. These should be oral presentations which have been assigned, researched, and prepared in outline form in advance of the actual debate.)

Glossary for Lesson One
Basic Factors in Business

Accounting: a system of recording and summarizing business and financial transactions and analyzing, verifying, and reporting the results.

You did not receive the proper payment due to an *accounting* error.

Agriculture: farming, raising livestock, producing crops.

Agriculture is an important industry in California.

Bankrupt: unable to pay one's debts and legally freed from the responsibility of paying them.

After suffering losses for years, the business finally went *bankrupt*.

Bond: an interest-bearing certificate of public or private indebtedness.

Both the government and utility companies borrow money by issuing *bonds*.

Capital: money or property and equipment used for production.

The company can raise *capital* by issuing new stock.

The company has made *capital* improvements by purchasing new machinery and equipment.

Creditor: one to whom the business owes money.

If the company has a successful year and good profits, they will be able to pay their *creditors*.

Debt: an amount of money which must be paid to someone.

By selling his business, he was able to pay off all his *debts*.

Distributing: refers to transportation, storage, and delivery of products from the point of production to the place where they can be sold.

The products are available in supermarkets across the country because of nationwide *distributing* methods.

Employee: a person who works for another person or a business, especially for money.

General Motors Corporation has several thousand *employees*.

Employer: a person or company that hires workers and provides work.

That drug company is one of the largest *employers* of chemists.

Boeing is one of the largest *employers* in Seattle.

The *employer* provides medical insurance and a retirement plan in addition to excellent wages.

Entrepreneur: a person who starts, manages, and takes the risks of running a business.

The tourist industry provides opportunities for many small *entrepreneurs* who operate shops and restaurants.

Extract: to separate part of something by physical or chemical process.

Salt is *extracted* from sea water.

The iron was *extracted* from the ore.

Finance: to provide money for the purchase of something or the operation of a business.

The company can *finance* its expansion by issuing more stock.

I *financed* my new car with a loan from the bank.

Industrialized: refers to having industries, particularly modern factories which produce goods for sale.

The leaders of the *industrialized* countries met in Canada.

Initiate: to begin something new.

That bank will *initiate* a new type of savings account designed to attract small investors.

Innovative: new, particularly referring to a new idea, method or device.

They have an *innovative* method of management which has resulted in improved productivity.

Insurance policy: a contract whereby one party, the insurer, agrees to guarantee another, the policy holder, against certain losses.

An automobile *insurance policy* will pay for medical expenses and damage to the automobile in the event of an accident.

Loss: the amount by which the cost and expenses exceeds the income.

Our business suffered a *loss* last year because we were unable to raise prices enough to cover expenses.

Mental: refers to use of the mind, thinking.

Because of modern machines and technology more and more *mental* work is required of employees who must be trained to operate the machines.

Merchandising: business activity related to buying and selling of goods.

Department stores and supermarkets are examples of *merchandising* enterprises.

Physical: related to the body and use of muscles to produce something which can be perceived by the senses.

Farming has always involved hard *physical* labor.

Policy: (see also *insurance policy*) a principle, method or rule which determines how an organization is operated.

It is the *policy* of this company that workers receive two weeks' paid vacation each year.

Product: something made or produced which is to be sold; goods, merchandise.

Paper and lumber are two of the *products* made from wood.

Production: the act of making goods for human wants; total output.

Petroleum is an important raw material for the *production* of plastics.

Profit: the amount by which income exceeds costs.

That company had a *profit* of $10,000,000 last year.

Provide: to make available to someone, to give, to sell.

This company *provides* work for ten thousand employees.

Raw materials: materials in their natural, unmanufactured condition.

Crude oil is the *raw material* from which gasoline is made.

Real estate: property in houses and land.

He borrowed money from the bank to purchase some *real estate*.

Risk: chance; in business, the possibility of failure.

Drilling for oil is an activity that involves considerable *risk*.

Robot: a machine which takes the place of humans for production purposes.

In automobile production *robots* are used to weld sections of the body.

Secure: (in this context) to bring about.

Corporations can *secure* capital by issuing bonds.

Service: business activity related to providing help, repair or assistance as opposed to selling or producing.

Business is the activity of producing and distributing goods and *services*.

Stock: any of the equal parts that the ownership of a corporation is divided into.

The corporation issued more *stock* to finance the expansion.

Venture: a business activity or undertaking, especially one that involves some risk or danger of a loss.

This individual is seeking partners for a joint *venture* in gas exploration.

Introduction to Lesson Two:
Legal Forms of Organization

Lesson Two deals with three basic forms of business ownership. Two different approaches are used to present this text. First, the types of business ownership are described using definitions and explanations as in the previous lesson. Second, the different forms of business ownership are compared and contrasted. The advantages and disadvantages of each form are included in the comparison and contrast.

The student should be aware of the compare and contrast method for determining the meanings of new vocabulary through context. The meanings of new vocabulary can be inferred from its similarity to or difference from known words and concepts. The vocabulary exercises concentrate on deriving meanings through comparison, contrast, and inference. The second reading of the material should find the reader actively using these methods.

Much of the vocabulary in this lesson is related to the legal aspects of business, and the reader should be aware that these words are defined and explained specifically in their business and legal context. Since these words may have other more common meanings, it is important to learn to understand vocabulary from the context rather than relying on the dictionary.

The vocabulary exercises in this chapter require not only analysis of the words to determine roots and suffixes, but also analysis of sentences to determine the parts of speech.

Linguistic concepts important for this lesson are suffixes, parts of speech, antonyms, conjunctions and other transition elements, topic sentences, and comparatives.

At the New York Stock Exchange traders execute *buy* and *sell* orders for stock of large corporations. Stockholders buy, sell, and trade without permission of other owners.

Legal Forms of Organization

How a Business Is Organized

Paragraph 1

permitted by law In business there are many <u>legal</u> forms of organization. The form of organization means the type of ownership. The main differences between the types of ownership are in their ability to raise capital, the size **business; use** and continuity of the <u>enterprise</u>, the <u>disposition</u> of profits, and the legal **requirements; case** <u>obligations</u> in the <u>event</u> of bankruptcy. Each form has certain advantages and disadvantages. The three forms discussed in this lesson are the sole proprietorship, the partnership, and the corporation.

Paragraph 2

The form which requires the least amount of capital and personnel is the sole proprietorship. Sole means single, and the proprietor is the owner. Therefore, a sole proprietorship is a business owned and operated by a single person. This single person can start a business by simply purchasing the necessary goods and equipment and <u>opening up shop</u>. **rules; follow** There are very few government and legal <u>regulations</u> to <u>comply with</u>. **property** The sole proprietor owns all the business <u>assets</u>, makes all the decisions,

19

takes all the risks, and keeps all the profits of the business. The business itself pays no tax, but the owner must pay personal income taxes on his profits. If a sole proprietor is successful, he takes a lot of personal satisfaction in his enterprise. If he is not successful and he wants to close

products or supplies   his business and start a new one, he simply has to sell his <u>inventory</u> and equipment, pay his bills, <u>close up shop</u>, and begin a new activity.

Paragraph 3

things to consider   There are good and bad <u>aspects</u> to the sole proprietorship form of organization. The sole proprietor has the opportunity to be successful,

takes a chance on   but he also <u>runs the risk of financial ruin</u>. The sole proprietor owns all
losing all his money   the assets of the business, but he also has to supply all the <u>capital</u>, and
money   his ability to borrow is limited to his personal amount of money and

property   <u>wealth</u>. The owner enjoys his freedom to make decisions about his business, but he alone takes the responsibility for incorrect choices. He

must pay;   has the right to keep all the profits of the business. However, if he suffers
responsibility   a loss, he still <u>owes</u> all the debts, and his legal <u>liability</u> to pay them may be more than his investment in the business. He must use his personal

pay   property to <u>settle</u> the debts of the business if he goes bankrupt.

Paragraph 4

A partnership presents a completely different set of problems. A partnership consists of two or more people who share the ownership of a business. A partnership should begin with a legal agreement covering

parts   the various <u>aspects</u> of the business. Two important items that need to be
property; investing   covered are exactly which <u>assets</u> each partner is <u>contributing</u>, as well as
ended   how the partnership can be changed or <u>terminated</u>. This agreement is called the articles of co-partnership. It is not as complicated as the

show   articles of incorporation. However, the articles of co-partnership <u>indi-</u>
beginning   <u>cate</u> that the <u>initiation</u> of a partnership is not as easy as the beginning of a sole proprietorship. Partners are like sole proprietors because they own all the assets, owe all the debts, make the decisions, and share the profits. They pay only personal income taxes on their share of the

knowledge   profits. If each partner has a different <u>expertise</u> in an important business
the talents of the   area, the partnership has an advantage over the sole proprietorship in
people who run   <u>managerial ability</u>.
the business

Paragraph 5

A partnership usually has more capital than a sole proprietorship. In a
get   partnership the personal wealth of all the partners can be used to <u>secure</u>
pay   loans and credit. This personal wealth may also be used to <u>settle</u> the debts of the business. Like the sole proprietorship, the partnership has

total responsibility	unlimited financial liability in the event of bankruptcy. Unlike the sole proprietorship where one owner-manager makes all the decisions, the
rules; stop	smooth operation of a partnership requires both owners to agree on management policy. If a partnership wished to cease doing business, the
break up	owners would have to agree on how to dissolve it.

Paragraph 6

<table>
<tr><td>organization</td><td rowspan="2">The corporation is very different from both a sole proprietorship and a partnership. First of all, the corporation is a legal <u>entity</u> which is</td></tr>
<tr><td>made legal; formed</td></tr>
</table>

The corporation is very different from both a sole proprietorship and a partnership. First of all, the corporation is a legal entity which is

organization	The corporation is very different from both a sole proprietorship and a
made legal; formed	partnership. First of all, the corporation is a legal entity which is chartered by the state in which it is incorporated. In other words, a Los Angeles corporation is incorporated under the laws of the State of California. As a legal entity, the corporation can own property that is not the personal wealth of its owners. It also means that the corporation can enter into business agreements on its own. Forming a corporation is
steps	not easy. There are many legal procedures to follow. A corporation raises capital in a different way from the proprietorship or partnership.
parts of ownership	The ownership of the corporation is divided into shares of stock. One
owner	stockholder or shareowner can buy, sell, and trade his shares without permission from the other owners. A corporation can raise large amounts of capital by selling shares of stock. The stock owners vote for a board of
group	directors who hire a president or chief executive officer to run the company. The board of directors also decides what to do with the
keeps	corporation's profits. It usually retains part of the profits for reinvest-
pays out	ment in the company and distributes the other part to the shareholders
may not be	as dividends. Unlike the sole proprietorship and the partnership, the
more than	liability of a corporation is limited to the value of the assets of the company. The personal wealth of the stockholders cannot be used to pay debts in case of bankruptcy. Corporations do not operate like other
changed	forms of business because the ownership can be easily transferred through stock sales.

Paragraph 7

think about	There are favorable and unfavorable points to consider with regard to
can use	the corporate form of ownership. The corporation has access to large amounts of capital and has limited liability, but its activities are closely
watched	monitored by government agencies. The Securities and Exchange Commission regulates the stock trades. A large corporation has a lot of managers who can specialize in different aspects of the business. How-
good	ever, the corporation must have good organization for efficient operation. Another important disadvantage of the corporation is that its profits are taxed twice. The profits are taxed once as corporate profits, and then the individual stockholders pay personal income taxes on their
profits from stocks	dividends.

Paragraph 8

The three types of legal organization discussed in this lesson show different possibilities and limitations. The best form for a particular enterprise depends on its capital requirements and the number of owners.

Vocabulary Building Introduction

Sometimes the meaning of a new word can be learned by analyzing the word. Analysis means looking at the different parts of something. The word *ownership*, for example, is made up of the verb *own* followed by two suffixes, *-er* and *-ship*. Sometimes when a suffix is added to a word, the spelling is changed. Close analysis of the word will show its parts.

A: Word analysis

Read Paragraph 1 and make a list of the words which are formed with the suffixes: *-ation, -tion, -ent, -ence, -ity,* and *-ship.*

Which of these words are used as nouns? Analysis of the sentences will reveal the different parts of the sentences: the subjects, the verbs, etc.

B: Vocabulary fill-ins

Paragraphs 1 and 2 contain several nouns which are derived from verbs. Read Paragraph 2. Study the nouns and the verb forms listed below.

differ	difference	own	owner, ownership
continue	continuity	decide	decision
equip	equipment	satisfy	satisfaction
bankrupt	bankruptcy		

In the following sentences supply the correct verb or noun from the list above.

1. The sole proprietor can _____ for himself if he wants to form a new business.

2. The _____ can keep all of the profits of the business.

3. The proprietor made a _____ to purchase some new _____ .

4. The sole proprietorship, partnership, and corporation _____ in the manner in which they raise capital.

5. If the owner makes the wrong decision, it may _____ the business.

6. The proprietor doesn't wish to _____ his enterprise, because he has been unsuccessful and he doesn't get any _____ from his efforts.

7. It takes capital to purchase inventory and _____ the workshop with the necessary tools.

8. We try to _____ the customers so that they will _____ to shop here.

C: Vocabulary in context

Word meaning can be determined by the sentence. The following sentences indicate the meaning of the word directly as in a definition or indirectly by means of another element of the sentence. Read the following sentences and try to understand the meanings by using the context.

1. A *sole proprietorship* is a business owned and operated by one person.
2. The business operator must *comply with* the legal regulations. (Hint: What do you do with regulations? You either *obey* them or *break* them.)
3. The sole proprietor *purchases* the goods and equipment. The sole proprietor owns all the *assets*. (Hint: After he purchases, he owns.)
4. When he terminates his business, he simply sells the *inventory* and equipment. (Hint: Contrast this sentence with No. 3.)
5. If he is successful, he takes a lot of personal satisfaction in his *enterprise*. If he is unsuccessful, he might decide to close up shop.
6. His ability to *borrow* capital is determined by his personal wealth because his *personal wealth* serves as collateral to guarantee the loan.
7. He *is entitled* to keep all the profits of the business.
8. His *personal property* can be used to *settle* the debts. (Hint: What does a person do about his debts?)
9. He *appreciates* his freedom to make business decisions.
10. He *bears the responsibility* (is responsible for) his business decisions.

D: Matching

Match the expressions to others with similar meanings.

1. appreciates	_____ a. takes blame or credit for
2. comply with	_____ b. one-owner business
3. sole proprietorship	_____ c. things of value to a business
4. purchases	_____ d. goods
5. assets	_____ e. business
6. inventory	_____ f. go out of business
7. close up shop	_____ g. follow
8. is entitled	_____ h. is allowed by law
9. enterprise	_____ i. buys
10. bears responsibility for	_____ j. enjoys
11. borrow	_____ k. things he owns besides his business
12. personal property	_____ l. use something which belongs to someone else

E: Multiple choice

Many of the sentences and paragraphs in this lesson compare or contrast certain aspects of business ownership; that is, they point to similarities or differences. For example, in Paragraph 2 two successive sentences begin: "If the sole proprietor is successful . . ." and "If he is not successful . . ." These two sentences begin with introductory clauses, one affirmative and one negative. They are opposites, so we might expect the results of these conditions to be opposite as well. Paragraph 4 contains the sentence: "Partners are like sole proprietors because they both own all the assets, owe all the debts . . ." This sentence emphasizes similarities in the two forms of ownership. There are many words and phrases which indicate comparisons and contrasts to the reader or listener.

Words and Phrases Indicating Comparisons	Words and Phrases Indicating Contrasts
in addition	but
also	while
and	although
together	not as
as	unlike
like	different
furthermore	on the other hand
both	however
another	
as well as	

Sometimes these words can help us guess the meaning of new vocabulary since when we hear or read them, we can expect to find either two comparable ideas or two contrasting ideas.

In the following sentences, try to determine the meanings of the underlined words from the context. Try to think of contrasts or opposites. Select the word which most nearly means the same as the underlined word.

1. The sole proprietor is liable for all the debts of his enterprise. He owns all the assets, but he owes all the <u>liabilities</u>.

   a. inventory   c. capital
   b. proprietorship   d. debts

2. The different forms of organization are taxed differently on their profits. They also have different legal obligations with regard to their debts in the <u>event</u> of bankruptcy.

   a. case   c. cost
   b. aspect   d. failure

3. His personal <u>assets</u> can be used to settle the debts.

   a. wealth   c. freedom
   b. capital   d. inventory

4. The articles of co-partnership explain how the partnership is started and how it should be <u>dissolved</u>.

   a. initiated   c. ended
   b. sold   d. regulated

5. When the sole proprietor stops doing business, he simply sells his inventory and <u>equipment</u>.

   a. labor   c. debts
   b. machines for making   d. profits
      goods

6. In addition to the benefits of running a sole proprietorship, there are also some <u>unfavorable aspects</u>.

   a. profits   c. assets
   b. disadvantages   d. satisfaction

7. He has freedom to make his own decisions, but he <u>bears sole responsibility</u> for errors when he makes a wrong choice.

   a. profits   c. takes all the blame
   b. loses   d. does not have freedom

8. His responsibility for debt can be greater than his <u>investment</u> in the business.

   a. partnership   c. profits
   b. assets   d. capital

9. A partnership does not have some of the <u>disadvantages</u> of a sole proprietorship, but it shares some similarities.

   a. benefits   c. agreement
   b. problems   d. association

10. If the owners of a partnership wished to stop doing business, both <u>managers</u> would have to agree on how to dissolve the partnership.

   a. partners   c. shops
   b. corporations   d. profits

Listening and Note-Taking Skills

F: Outlining

Below are the headings for a short outline of Paragraph 2. Listen to or read Paragraph 2 and using the following major headings, draw up an outline and fill in the details.

The Sole Proprietorship

A. Definition; B. Starting the Sole Proprietorship; C. Operating the Business; D. The Successful Business; E. The Unsuccessful Business.

G: Organizing information into categories

Paragraph 3 explains more about the sole proprietorship. Each of the sentences has at least two parts which contrast the advantages of this form of business with the disadvantages. Make two columns, one headed *Advantages* and the other *Disadvantages*, and list these from the sentences in Paragraph 3 under their appropriate heading.

H: Analyzing a paragraph

A good writer introduces the main topic of the text in the first paragraph. In the introductory paragraph, the author said he would discuss three legal forms of organization. What were they?

I: Outlining by noticing parallelism

Paragraphs 2 and 3 discussed the first form of legal organization. You have already outlined those two paragraphs. Next listen to Paragraphs 4 and 5. They are similar in organization to Paragraphs 2 and 3. Paragraph 4 discusses the definition, formation, and operation of the partnership, and Paragraph 5 discusses some of the advantages and disadvantages. We refer to this similarity in form as parallel development. Write outlines of Paragraphs 4 and 5 (e.g., 4. Partnerships; and 5. Advantages and Disadvantages of Partnerships).

Reading Comprehension

J: Comprehension questions

Paragraph 6 discusses the corporation. You have noticed that the discussions of the sole proprietorship and the partnership had some similarities of form. The outlines parallel each other. Read the following questions about Paragraph 6.

1. From the first sentence do you expect that the discussion of the corporations will parallel the discussions of the sole proprietorship and partnership in form?
2. Are the other two forms of legal organization more similar to each other than to the corporate form of ownership?
3. What is a difference in the way a corporation raises capital?
4. What happens to the profits of a corporation?
5. How can a stockholder terminate his interest in a corporation?
6. If a corporation goes bankrupt, how does this differ from the bankruptcy of a sole proprietorship or partnership?
7. What is a problem associated with the size of a corporation?

Vocabulary Review: Rephrasing

K: Rephrasing words

Rewrite the following sentences. Replace the words *in italics* with expressions from the text which have the same meaning.

1. The *sole proprietor* may keep all the profits derived from his *business*.
2. A sole proprietorship is the easiest to *initiate* and the easiest to *terminate*.
3. There is the *opportunity* to be successful, but also the owner *takes a chance* on financial ruin.
4. His personal *assets* can be used to *pay* the debts in the *event* of bankruptcy.

5. The *joint owners* owe all the *liabilities* and pay personal income taxes on their *part* of the profits.

6. The ability to *borrow money* is greater in a partnership because the personal *property* of the partners can be used to get a loan.

7. In the case of *business failure,* the *responsibility* of the corporation for its debts is limited.

8. The board of directors *keeps* part of the profits to *increase the capital* of the corporation.

9. The *stockholders* pay personal income taxes on their *profits from stock.*

10. The activities of the corporation are closely *watched* by the government.

Writing

L: Writing and organizing a paragraph

The topic sentence of a paragraph tells us what the paragraph is about. It should state the ideas which are going to be discussed in the paragraph. The last sentence is often a summary. Sometimes the concluding sentence of a paragraph does not only summarize what has been said, but may also point out another side of the topic which has not been discussed.

Write a paragraph emphasizing the similarities between a sole proprietorship and a partnership. In your first, or topic sentence, write what the similarities are. Then write two sentences about each similarity. Conclude your paragraph by mentioning that besides these similarities, there are some differences.

Oral Practice

Debate

Resolved: It is better for all types of businesses to be incorporated and have limited liability. (Discuss the arguments for and against this statement.)

Glossary for Lesson Two
Legal Forms of Organization

Ability: a skill or a talent; the capacity or capability to do something.
He has the *ability* to type 60 words per minute.

This company has the *ability* to increase production using the present equipment.

Because of my experience as a banker, I have the *ability* to make financial decisions.

Access: the means of getting to something.

A corporation has a greater *access* to capital than does a sole proprietor.

Articles of co-partnership: the agreement telling the terms and conditions of a partnership.

The *articles of co-partnership* should also provide a method of selling the business.

Articles of incorporation: the agreement telling the terms, conditions and purposes of a corporation. These must be filed in the state where the corporation is chartered.

My lawyer will draw up the *articles of incorporation*.

Asset: (often plural) anything of value to a company. Anything which can be sold or converted into cash.

The partners each own a share of the *assets* of the partnership.

Inventory is a current *asset* because it will be sold during that business year.

Bankrupt: unable to pay one's debts and legally released from the liability.

His business went *bankrupt* because of poor management and bad financial decisions.

Bills: debts; money which must be paid to someone for a service or product received.

The *bill* for my telephone service arrives today.

Most suppliers want you to pay the *bill* within thirty days.

Board of directors: a group of persons elected by stockholders to run a corporation.

The *board of directors* has decided to pay a dividend of $5 per share.

Capital: the money which owners or stockholders invest in a business.

We need some *capital* in order to purchase new production equipment.

Chief executive officer (CEO): the top manager or director of a company.

The board of directors has hired a new *chief executive officer* for the corporation.

Comply: obey

The corporation must *comply* with all the regulations which pertain to it.

Corporation: a group of persons granted a charter to do business as a separate unit with its own rights and responsibilities.

Large businesses are operated as *corporations* because capital can be easily raised and liability is limited.

Dissolve: to break up a partnership or corporation.

The partnership was *dissolved* because the two partners wanted to have their own businesses.

Dividends: a share of the profits of a corporation which is given to the stockholders.

The *dividend* will be paid to owners of record on June 30.

Enterprise: a business, particularly one privately owned.

If the sole proprietor wants to quit, he can simply find someone to purchase his *enterprise.*

Entity: a separate unit for ownership or legal purposes.

As a separate *entity* a corporation can own property apart from the individual stockholders.

Equipment: machinery or tools which a business uses for production and operation.

By using new *equipment,* the company hopes to be able to increase production and reduce costs.

Expertise: special knowledge or ability.

This accountant has *expertise* in financial planning.

Financial: refers to money or the management of money.

This company is in good *financial* condition.

The sole proprietor makes all his own *financial* decisions.

Income tax: a tax which is based on the amount of money a person or company receives for labor, services, or products, and which cannot be added to the price of the labor, services, or products.

The owner of a sole proprietorship pays personal *income tax* on the profit he receives. The business itself pays no tax.

Inventory: the amount of goods, merchandise, or materials on hand.

Once each year the owners of the store must record all their *inventory* in order to know which goods they have on hand.

Some new computerized cash registers are able to keep track of *inventory.*

Liability: (often plural) debt or legal responsibility.

The assets and *liabilities* of the company must be listed on the balance sheet.

The *liability* of a corporation is limited to its assets.

The sole proprietor has all the *liabilities* of his business.

Limited: restricted; not allowed to exceed a certain amount.

A corporation's liability is *limited* to the value of its assets.

Ownership: refers to a right a person has to things that belong to him.

The *ownership* of a sole proprietorship can be transferred if the proprietor wants to sell it.

In order to sell a car, you must have an *ownership* certificate.

Private *ownership* of property is an American tradition.

Partnership: a business owned by two or more individuals.

The owners of a *partnership* share in the operation and profits of the business.

Profits: the amount of income above costs.

The *profits* have increased due to a decrease in the cost of raw materials.

Proprietorship: ownership of a small business.

This restaurant is operated as a sole *proprietorship*. It is owned by one individual.

Purchase: buy.

The individual owner can decide whether or not to *purchase* new tools and equipment.

Satisfaction: a feeling of pleasure or contentment.

Many small businessmen have the *satisfaction* of being their own bosses.

Securities and Exchange Commission (SEC): the government commission designed to protect individuals who purchase shares of stock from publicly held companies.

A copy of the corporation's balance sheet must be filed with the *SEC*.

Introduction to Lesson Three: Production

In Lesson Three, as in previous lessons, there are definitions and explanations contained in the text which elaborate the meanings of the words. While the forms of ownership in Lesson Two shared some common characteristics, the two methods of production discussed here have opposite methods and purposes. Students should develop their ability to discern meanings by contrasting known words with unknown ones. The meanings of the words used to describe each method of production contrast as sharply as the methods themselves; for example, *continuous* as opposed to *intermittent*.

Many vocabulary items in this lesson can be changed from nouns to verbs or adjectives by means of suffixes. The vocabulary exercises require the students to become familiar with these suffixes and to use them. For example, in changing the words from nouns to verbs, the student is required to analyze the structure of the sentences as well as the structure of the words.

Finally, many explanations in this chapter employ examples to illustrate meanings. This use of examples assists students in learning to order ideas according to importance. On the second reading the students should be aware of general ideas incorporated in topic sentences and the examples that follow. By concentrating on the two methods of production and systematizing ideas according to each of the methods, students are encouraged to develop their analytical skills and increase comprehension and retention.

Linguistic concepts important for the student to work with this lesson are: parts of speech, suffixes, synonyms, parallels, and spelling rules for suffixes.

Labor (workers) and capital (tools) complete the fabrication of computers at Apple Computer Inc.

Employees and machines perform their operations on the product as it moves along an assembly line from start to finish.

An advantage of the assembly line is that finished products roll off the line at one point where they can be quickly and easily stacked.

3

Production

The Two Basic Methods of Production

Paragraph 1

Production is the process of making something of value. It means bringing together materials, machinery, and workers to make goods. Production changes the value of materials by changing their form. The process of production makes the materials more valuable.

Paragraph 2

There are four types of production: analysis, synthesis, extraction, and fabrication. Analysis is the process of separating a raw material into several parts. For example, in petroleum refining, oil is separated into gasoline, kerosene, fuel oil, asphalt, and many other products. Synthesis is the process of putting together two or more raw materials into one finished product. For example, glass is made by joining together lime, soda, potash, and other chemicals. All of the raw materials used in
taken production are <u>extracted</u> from the land, the sea, or the air. Mining and petroleum production extract raw materials from the earth. Fish and

minerals such as magnesium, sodium, chlorine, and bromine are extracted from the sea. Nitrogen and oxygen are extracted from the air. Fabrication is the process of making products of more value from already manufactured materials. The materials may be cut, machined, woven, knitted, shaped, or put together with other materials. For example, cloth is made from thread. Automobiles are made from already manufactured parts.

Paragraph 3

There are two basic methods of production: intermittent and continuous. In intermittent production, several of the same type of items are produced. Then production of that item stops and production of another item begins. Labor and equipment work on one particular product for a short period of time. The company makes a product either because a customer has ordered it or because they think a customer will order it. Machinery is set up and adjusted for a specific job. When the job is finished, the machinery is taken apart or reset for a different job.

Paragraph 4

With intermittent production many designs and styles are possible, so a large variety of goods can be produced. The design can easily be changed to suit each individual customer. When goods are made to customer specifications, they are called custom-made. Only a limited number, perhaps only one, of each specification are made. Therefore, automatic machines have limited use, and increased labor is necessary, which makes custom-made goods expensive. However, one of the reasons that custom-made goods are popular is that they are expensive; if someone owns one, it shows that he has money.

Paragraph 5

In continuous production, labor and equipment work continuously, making one type of product for a long period of time. The company buys specialized machinery, or they adjust their machinery for a production period that will probably continue for months. The products **uniform** must be <u>standardized</u> and the volume must be large. The assembly line method of manufacturing is one way of using continuous production. Coordination is more necessary in continuous production than in intermittent production, because if there is a break at any step in production, it can halt the whole process.

Paragraph 6

changeable

Continuous production is generally less <u>flexible</u> than intermittent production. Standardization is necessary in order to get the greatest benefit from continuous production. Therefore, there can be only a few models, styles, and designs. To say it another way, if the number of models and styles of a product increases, the volume must also increase in order to use the continuous process efficiently. Because the major automobile manufacturers have a very large volume of production, they can produce several body designs, engine sizes, and style series and still use the continuous process of manufacturing. In addition to car manufacturers, many other factories use continuous production. For example, it is used in making consumer appliances, producing cement, making paper, refining sugar, refining petroleum, weaving cloth, and grinding grain.

Paragraph 7

Standard goods are generally manufactured using the continuous type of production process. They are made to the manufacturer's specifications, not the customer's. In order to sell goods, it is necessary to make items that the customers will buy; however, standard goods are made not for a specific customer, but for a group of customers. We can say that standard design tries to please the average taste. When a large volume of

have stamped
on them
name

each design is produced, as a practical matter it is necessary to make goods to suit the average customer. Standard goods usually <u>carry</u> the manufacturer's <u>brand</u> and are advertised over a large area to reach many customers.

Paragraph 8

In deciding on the type of production to use in a plant, the important factors are volume and the number of models and designs. Intermittent production can be used if volume is small or there are many designs. Often a company begins production with job lots using intermittent production. As the company grows and the volume increases, it is more efficient to use continuous production.

Vocabulary Building Introduction

A: Parts of speech

The following groups of words are all related in meaning because they have the same roots. Notice the different suffixes indicating different parts of speech.

Verb	Noun	Adjective
continue	continuation	continuous
standardize	standardization	standard
assemble	assembly	
extract	extraction	
produce	product	productive
synthesize	synthesis	synthetic
analyze	analysis	analytic
manufacture	manufacturer	manufactured
proceed	process	
specify	specification	specific

Read the following sentences carefully and supply the correct form of the word.

continue
1. In _____ production labor and equipment work nonstop, producing a high volume of standard products.

assemble
2. The _____ line was first used by Henry Ford for _____ automobiles.

standard
3. _____ parts are produced by the manufacturer because he believes that someone will buy them. The _____ of parts enabled manufacturers to produce in a continuous process.

extract
4. The _____ of oil from underneath the ocean floor requires expensive equipment.

produce
5. The continuous process is a much more _____ method of manufacturing certain goods than the intermittent process.

synthesize
6. Many _____ products are made from oil.

analyze
7. By means of _____ many important fuels can be produced from crude oil.

manufacturer
8. These items were _____ in Switzerland.

proceed
9. We shall use the new _____ developed by our research staff.

specific
10. The customer _____ how he wanted the product designed. We must build it to his _____.

B: Vocabulary in context

The following sentences indicate the meaning of the word directly as in a definition or indirectly by means of another element of the sentence. Read the following sentences and try to understand the meanings by using the context.

1. <u>Production</u> involves bringing together workers, machinery, and <u>raw materials</u> to make <u>goods.</u>

2. Through <u>analysis</u>, gasoline, kerosene, fuel oil, asphalt, and many other products are obtained from oil.

3. Glass is <u>synthesized</u> by joining together lime, soda, potash, and other raw materials.

4. Some raw materials, such as coal and copper ore, are <u>extracted</u> from the earth.

5. The <u>fabrication</u> of automobiles <u>involves</u> the assembly of previously manufactured parts.

6. Using the <u>intermittent</u> method of production, a manufacturer sets his machinery to produce a certain number of units, a <u>job lot</u>. When the job is finished, the machinery is reset to produce different items to fill another order.

7. Goods produced to suit individual customers are called <u>custom-made</u>.

8. In <u>continuous</u> production, the machinery is set to produce identical products for a long period of time.

9. Continuous production of identical items is made possible by <u>standardization</u> of parts.

10. In production, <u>volume</u> refers to the number of units produced in a given period of time.

11. To keep production most <u>efficient</u>, we need to produce the highest volume using the least amount of machines and labor.

12. <u>Standard goods</u> are designed to please the average taste.

Now rewrite the above sentences substituting one of the words or phrases from the list below for the underlined words.

chemical breakdown	output
factory operation	produced
fitting together	production
cost effective	production models
interchangeability and uniformity	single order
	specially designed
mined	start-and-stop
nonstop or assembly line	products
unmanufactured elements	manufacture

Listening and Note-Taking Skills

C: Topic sentences

Listen to Paragraph 1. In one sentence state its main idea.

D: Outlining

Paragraph 2 begins with a topic sentence naming the four types of production. Listen to Paragraph 2 and outline it.

Reading Comprehension

E: Organizing information into categories

Paragraphs 3, 4, 5, and 6 discuss the differences between intermittent and continuous production. Read these paragraphs and list the contrasting aspects.

F: Multiple choice

Read Paragraphs 6, 7, and 8. Then look at the sentences below and select the word which best explains the underlined word.

1. In continuous production labor and equipment work continuously making one type of product.
    a. unit.   c. job.
    b. style.   d. material.

2. Products must be standardized and the volume must be large.
    a. number of units. c. cost.
    b. loudness.   d. efficiency.

3. Coordination is more necessary in continuous production than in intermittent production.
    a. efficiency.   c. design.
    b. control of all   d. standardization.
       aspects of
       manufacturing.

4. Continuous production is less flexible than intermittent production.
    a. efficient.   c. expensive.
    b. adaptable.   d. standardized.

5. Standardization is necessary in order to get the greatest <u>benefit</u> from continuous production.

    a. advantage.   c. series.
    b. output.   d. style.

6. If the number of styles increases, the volume must also increase in order to use this process <u>efficiently</u>.

    a. inexpensively.   c. advantageously.
    b. generally.   d. easily.

7. The large automobile manufacturers produce several body <u>designs</u>.

    a. styles.   c. volumes.
    b. automobiles.   d. series.

8. Continuous production is used in making <u>consumer</u> appliances.

    a. for the home.   c. expensive.
    b. industrial.   d. customer.

9. Standard goods are made according to the manufacturer's <u>specifications</u>.

    a. process.   c. volume.
    b. design details.   d. customers.

10. Often a company begins production with <u>job lots</u> using intermittent production.

    a. one order of a   c. parking places.
       certain item.
    b. workers.   d. raw materials.

Writing

G: Writing a paragraph of contrast

Using the list of differences from the reading comprehension exercise (E), write one paragraph contrasting the production of custom and standard goods.

Vocabulary Review: Rephrasing

H: Rephrasing words

Rewrite the following sentences. Replace the words in *italics* with expressions from the text which have the same meaning.

1. Mining and petroleum production *take* raw materials from the earth.
2. In continuous production, the products must be similar and the *quantity* must be large.
3. Continuous production is used in making *appliances* for the home.
4. As production increases, it will become more *economical* to use continuous production.
5. Standard goods are made according to *what the manufacturer requires.*
6. Gasoline and kerosene are made by *separating* crude oil *into its component parts.*
7. *Assembly* is the process of putting together manufactured parts.
8. The company produces a product because a *buyer* has ordered it.
9. When goods are made to a customer's specifications, they are called *special orders.*
10. Using intermittent production, a manufacturer produces *one order.*

Oral Practice

Debate

Resolved: Prefabricated housing is the best answer to the increased costs of building houses. (Discuss the arguments for and against this. Be sure to deal with the problem of standardization in style.)

Glossary for Lesson Three
Production

Analysis: the separation of a whole into its various parts (components) so that the components are used as products.

Gasoline is produced from crude oil by *analysis.*

Appliance: an electrical household machine used for performing various kinds of housework.

Washing machines, vacuum cleaners, and refrigerators are examples of *appliances.*

New electrical *appliances* are designed to consume less energy.

Consumer: a person who purchases a product for his own personal use.

Standard products are designed to please the average *consumer.*

Consumers had to spend more money for food last month because of increased farm prices.

Continuous: nonstop, without interruption (for the purpose of resetting machinery).

Large manufacturers, who have lots of production machinery and can assign one machine for a particular job, use the *continuous* method of production. The machines can run for long periods, producing identical items without having to be reset.

Coordination: control and orderly arrangement of workers, machines, and materials working together efficiently.

To use the continuous method of production, it is necessary to have good *coordination* of workers, materials, and machines.

Custom-made: specially made for a particular customer, according to the customer's specifications.

A wealthy person can afford to have *custom-made* clothes.

Design: the arrangement of parts or details according to plan.

The machinery must be reset in order to change the *design* of the product.

Efficiently: using the least amount of energy and materials to produce the greatest output.

The Japanese produce cars *efficiently* by using the most modern methods and machinery.

Extraction: the process of removing raw materials from the "land" for the purpose of production.

Oil, metals, and other minerals are obtained through the process of *extraction*.

Fabrication: the assembly of manufactured parts.

Fabrication of modular units, which are standardized sections of buildings, is an inexpensive method of constructing new homes and offices.

Flexible: able to be bent back and forth or otherwise changed in some manner.

Springs are made from *flexible* steel.

Our production methods are *flexible* because it is easy to change the machines to produce different products.

Goods: manufactured products.

The Gross National Product (GNP) refers to the value of all the *goods* and services produced by a country.

Intermittent: starting and stopping, not operating continuously.

Small manufacturers that produce a variety of different products with the same machinery use *intermittent* production. After they produce one item, they must stop and adjust machinery before production of the next item can begin.

Job lot: a group of mass produced goods all manufactured at the same time to the same exact specifications.

This *job lot* contains fifty thousand women's dresses, size eight.

Machine: to turn, shape, plane, or mill using machine tools.

These pieces of steel will be *machined* into screws and nuts.

Production: the act of manufacturing or the volume of manufactured goods.

Production of 1982 model cars began on July 1, 1981.

Increased *production* will not result in increased profits unless sales can also be increased.

Raw materials: materials in their natural or unmanufactured state which will be synthesized or analyzed to produce marketable products.

Iron is one of the *raw materials* used in making steel.

Specifications: exact details of the dimensions, materials, and workmanship of a product.

These replacement parts are made to the original manufacturer's *specifications*.

Standard: refers to products designed for the general market, not for a particular individual.

These screws and nuts come in *standard* sizes.

This camera uses *standard* 35 mm film.

Standardized: refers to products all made exactly alike to a given set of specifications. Such products are interchangeable because they are exactly the same.

Electrical outlets in the United States are *standardized* so that the same appliance can be plugged into any outlet anywhere.

Electric light bulbs and sockets are *standardized* so that any light bulb can be screwed into any socket.

Style: design or fashion.

Clothing manufacturers change the *style* of their products every year.

People who want to wear clothes which are in *style* must purchase new clothes each year.

Synthesis: the combination of two raw materials for the purpose of producing a product.

Glass is produced by the *synthesis* of lime, soda, potash, and other chemicals.

Many modern textile fibers such as polyesters and nylon result from a *synthesis* of simple chemical compounds.

Volume: refers to the quantity produced in a certain amount of time.

High *volume* production can reduce the cost of each item produced.

It's not economical to produce a small *volume* of gasoline; millions of gallons are produced at once.

Introduction to Lesson Four:
Factory Layout

This lesson introduces some of the concepts necessary to understand and describe the general physical characteristics of the production facility. It deals with how the production methods relate to the factory design. Be sure to review the two basic methods of production before you begin this lesson.

Many vocabulary items in Lesson Four consist of words or phrases put together from smaller words or phrases. For example, the word *layout* is put together from *lay* and *out*. Sometimes the meanings of such compound words can be determined by looking at their different elements, but more often, the larger word or phrase has a meaning more related to some abstract meaning of the elements which make it up. For example, the word *bottleneck* has nothing to do with either a bottle or a neck, except as an abstract comparison. Be aware of these words and phrases as you learn the vocabulary, and notice the contrast between the meaning of the longer word or phrase and the meanings of its elements.

Since the topic of this lesson relates to that of the previous lesson, there is a good opportunity here for reinforcement and review of previously learned material. We know from Lesson One that *land* can mean the actual site or piece of real estate where production is carried out. Production machinery must be arranged to maximize output and minimize costs. The writing exercise in this lesson also emphasizes the methods of comparison and contrast and the organization of ideas required for the logical presentation of material.

Linguistic concepts useful for this chapter include compound words, comparison, and recognition and understanding of the passive voice.

Efficient use of space is demonstrated here where all positions are filled for the final assembly of the 737. A well-planned layout is arranged to maximize worker productivity and minimize cost.

4

Factory Layout

The Two Basic Types of Factory Layout

Paragraph 1

Layout is the arrangement of work space, equipment, products, rooms, doors, passageways, and so on in a place of business. In a well planned factory layout everything is arranged so that the product and workers move in an orderly manner and with the least possible confusion. Proper arrangement is necessary for smooth operation of the production system, the elimination of bottlenecks, and the minimum buildup of inventories and semi-finished products. A good layout should also take the worker into account so that there is a favorable working environment. An efficient layout helps to increase worker productivity and keep costs down by reducing walking distances for employees and keeping supervisors and maintenance personnel close to their areas of responsibility.

not allowing the system to slow down or stop

plan for the work

Paragraph 2

When planning a layout, the workers, the type of product and method of production, and the cost of space are all items which should be considered. It is much better to take the time to plan a good layout in the beginning than to have to change a poor one later. Plants and buildings cost a lot of money, and the cost is usually based on the amount of space involved. Efficient use of space is necessary in order to keep costs down. The modern practice, therefore, is to design the layout before the buildings are constructed. The buildings can then be designed to suit the layout. This is much more efficient than trying to design a layout to suit buildings already built.

Paragraph 3

Two general types of factory layout are associated with two basic methods of production. The continuous production method, which is used for petroleum, chemicals, and mass produced items such as automobiles and appliances, uses what is called a product layout. Intermittent production, used for example in a furniture factory and in general machine shops where there are several different products and

uses jobs, employs a process or functional layout.

Paragraph 4

With product layout the factory is set up to suit the particular product being manufactured. Employees and machines perform their operations on the product as it moves along an assembly line from start to finish. There are both advantages and disadvantages to this type of layout.

Paragraph 5

One advantage of product layout is that the use of assembly lines usually has lower unit costs than other methods have. The unit cost is the cost for producing one individual item. This lower unit cost can be

a result of attributed to a combination of factors. Machines and assembly lines can move the product through the production process quickly and effi-

used up ciently. Raw materials are consumed at fixed rates that are easily controlled. This makes large inventories and storage unnecessary. Another advantage is that by controlling and coordinating the use of machines, scheduling and routing are simplified so that bottlenecks are eliminated. Furthermore, finished products roll off the assembly line at one point

placed on a pallet where they can be easily and quickly stacked, palletized, loaded, and shipped. Finally, control and supervision are simplified by using product layout since each worker has a specific assignment on the line.

7/24

Paragraph 6

the whole line
stopping
changed to

A disadvantage of this type of layout is that a breakdown at any point on the assembly line usually results in a total shutdown of the line. Also, specialized machinery which is not easily adapted to other uses and uniform interchangeable parts are usually required for product layout. The result is that there are not many design changes or improvements

equipment
change; made
large output

which can be made to a product once production has started. Changes can be added only once a year when retooling is undertaken for the new models. A high volume is necessary to insure low unit costs, but the rate of production can be increased only by purchasing additional production equipment or by adding a second shift of workers. Finally, em-

attitude
repetitious
uncaring attitude
very little or no

ployee morale and workmanship can suffer because assembly line work is generally routine and boring. It is difficult for a worker to take personal pride in a mass produced product, and this alienation can result in a lack of job satisfaction.

Paragraph 7

Intermittent production employs a process or functional layout. In this type of layout, machines, materials, and workers are grouped according to the particular process each performs. In a furniture factory, for example, the cutting, gluing, and finishing or painting would all be done in different areas using different tools. In a machine shop, the

the machines
designed for
these purposes

grinding, sawing, drilling, and turning would be done in different areas on the appropriate machines. This type of layout also has advantages and disadvantages.

Paragraph 8

the ability to change

An advantage of process layout is that there is flexibility in the types of products manufactured, the assignments of workers, and the uses of machines. General purpose machines can be used for process layout,

do not need to be
changed as often
separately from
stop
lessen the problems
caused by one
machine depending
upon another
call their own

and these machines are usually less expensive and do not become obsolete as quickly as specialized assembly line machinery does. Machines operate independently of each other, and a breakdown of one machine would not result in a total line shutdown and, therefore, a complete halt in production. Different jobs are done in different areas; in this way interference is reduced. Furniture finishing, for example, must be done in a dust-free environment away from the saws and sanders. An advantage for workers is that they each have a specific job which they can identify with and take pride in.

Paragraph 9

A disadvantage of process layout is that there is no definite line in which materials move; therefore, they tend to move less efficiently. Special routing and cost analysis are necessary for each job order. Flexibility of
supply product demands that there be a larger inventory of raw materials, since
be different the amount of specific materials for each product or job order may vary. Generally, there is slower productivity with process layout, and pro-
a lot duction volume is restricted. If demand for a product increases substantially, it is often more efficient to change to product layout for a specific product.

Vocabulary Building Introduction

A: Vocabulary in context

Determining Meaning from Context
The following sentences indicate the meaning of the underlined word either directly, as in a definition, or indirectly by means of another element in the sentence. Read the following sentences and try to understand their meanings from the context.

1. Layout refers to the arrangement of workspace and equipment in a factory.

2. Production equipment refers to the tools and machinery used in the manufacturing process.

3. A bottleneck exists where raw materials or semi-finished products collect or bunch up at a point on the production line because they arrive there at a faster rate than they can be processed and moved on. Work is crowded together at a bottleneck. It does not continue smoothly on its route.

4. We want to reduce production because we have large inventories of unsold products. We should also reduce our purchasing since we have large inventories of raw materials.

5. Continuous production is generally a more efficient method of manufacturing than intermittent production. We can produce more at a lower cost and use less labor.

6. Product layout refers to an arrangement of workspace and equipment for production of a specific product. Automobiles, appliances, and other mass produced identical products are manufactured on assembly lines using a product layout.

7. When the assembly line shuts down because of the failure of one part, the workers are idle.

8. Maintenance personnel regularly service the machines to ensure that they are in proper operating condition.

9. As the cars move along the assembly line, doors, engines, and windshields are installed at stations along the way. Henry Ford used the assembly line to bring the work to the worker. Each worker performed a separate job in the assembly of the car.

10. All the parts are uniform; that means they are all exactly the same, and the same tools and machines can be used to produce and assemble them. Producing parts by machine instead of by hand allows us to produce uniform parts. Uniform parts are exactly identical. In order for a nut to fit on a bolt, the threads must be uniform. The teeth of the gears must be uniform in order for them to operate smoothly.

11. Uniform parts are interchangeable. The wheel from a particular car will fit all the others of the same model, and one part can be substituted for another. All the lug nuts on a wheel are interchangeable. It doesn't matter which nut goes on which bolt. Radial tires and bias ply tires are not interchangeable. If the wrong tire is used, it can cause serious handling problems.

12. The assembly line is shut down while the company retools. Certain modifications and improvements are being made in the product. The equipment must be adjusted to produce next year's models.

13. Since the machinery is operating at maximum speed, production can be increased only by duplication of the assembly line. We have to purchase equipment exactly like the equipment we already have.

14. If the workers fear that a company may go bankrupt, they will not be very productive and their morale will be very low. When a company has been making good profits, which it shares with the workers, the employees feel good about their jobs. Then employee morale improves significantly, and productivity increases.

15. The first shift of workers begins at 8 a.m. and finishes at 4 p.m. The second shift begins at 4 p.m. and finishes at midnight. By adding a second shift, we have been able to double production.

16. When the total cost of operating the factory is divided by the total number of items produced, we can determine the unit cost. Continuous production usually results in lower unit cost.

17. Due to a scheduling error our gluing machine is unable to do this job for your department today. The scheduling of machinery in a furniture factory using intermittent production is the responsibility of the shop supervisor.

18. Routing refers to the path which products follow in the intermittent production process. In continuous production routing is handled by proper design of the assembly line.

19. Pallets are wooden frames on which the finished product is stacked. Pallets can easily be handled by forklifts. The use of pallets eases the loading and unloading of trucks. When products are packed in large containers, we say they are containerized. When the products reach the end of the assembly lines, they can be quickly and easily palletized.

20. An electrical failure caused a complete shutdown of the factory.

21. This machine was designed to produce truck tires. But it could be easily adapted to produce automobile tires or trailer tires.

22. Working on an assembly line sometimes can be very boring. The workers perform the same job for eight hours per day. It is very routine work.

B: Matching

Match the words in the first column with expressions of similar meaning in the second column.

1. obsolete   _____ a . repetitious and boring

2. assignment   _____ b . factory

3. layout   _____ c . change and adjust continuous production equipment

4. routine   _____ d . doubling of production, equipment, and workers

5. plant   _____ e . an attitude of not caring about the product

6. alienation   _____ f . how workers feel about their work

7. uniform   _____ g . a group of workers who start at 4 p.m.

8. interchangeable _____ h . production expenses divided by the number of items produced

9. retool   _____ i . changed to be used for another purpose

10. duplication   _____ j . plan for placement of machines and workers

11. morale   _____ k . duty

12. second shift   _____ l . raw materials and unsold products in
                                 storage

13. unit cost   _____ m. old fashioned

14. adapted   _____ n . exactly equal

15. inventory   _____ o . able to be substituted for another part

C: Completion

Supply the correct form of a word from the previous exercises to complete the sentences below.

1. Since the present equipment is producing at maximum speed, production can be increased only by _____ of the assembly line.

2. The machines are _____ during the week between Christmas and New Year's Day when all the employees are off.

3. _____ can be kept to a minimum by carefully planning production schedules and delivery dates.

4. We try to schedule maintenance procedures at night to avoid having to pay the line workers for _____ time. They cannot produce anything when the machines are being serviced.

5. If we could produce this product on an assembly line, we could reduce the _____.

6. The reason these two parts have different stock numbers is that they are produced by different manufacturers, but you can use either one since they are _____.

7. If American manufacturers change to the metric system, all industrialized countries will have a _____ system of measure.

8. The camera can be _____ for underwater use by sealing it in a watertight plastic case.

9. Every year about this time, the automobile factories shut down in order to _____ for production of next year's models.

10. Employee _____ has improved since the office has been redecorated. Productivity has also increased.

Listening and Note-Taking Skills

D: Outlining

Paragraphs 1 and 2 contain introductory material for the lesson. Paragraph 1 presents a definition of *layout* and states why it is important. Paragraph 2 discusses what to consider when planning a layout, the reasons to consider these factors, and the most efficient method. Write an outline of Paragraphs 1 and 2 as you listen to them.

Reading Comprehension

E: Comprehension questions

Paragraph 3 states that the two types of layout are associated with two methods of production. Read Paragraph 3 and answer the following questions.

1. What are the two methods of production discussed in Paragraph 3?
2. What type of layout is used for continuous production?
3. What products are manufactured using continuous production?
4. What type of layout is used for intermittent production?
5. What products are manufactured using intermittent production?

F: Multiple choice

Paragraph 4 defines *product layout* and introduces the discussion of the advantages and disadvantages. Read Paragraph 4 carefully and choose the best answer.

1. The term *set up* in the first sentence most nearly means
   a. stretched out.   c. planted.
   b. planned.   d. produced.

2. The term *to suit* in the first sentence most nearly means
    a. to adapt.   c. to produce.
    b. to accommodate.   d. to design.

3. The term *particular* in the first sentence most nearly means
    a. specific.   c. identical.
    b. circumstantial.   d. critical.

4. The word *perform* in the second sentence most nearly means
    a. act.   c. do.
    b. fulfill.   d. achieve.

5. The word *operation* most nearly means
    a. transaction.   c. mission.
    b. work.   d. effect.

6. The concluding sentence states that there are advantages and dis-advantages to this *type of layout*. Which type?
    a. product.   c. functional.
    b. process.   d. planned.

7. What does this last sentence suggest will be the next topic discussed?
    a. process layout.   c. the advantages of product layout.
    b. product layout.   d. the disadvantages of process layout.

G: Main idea and details

The topic of a paragraph is the main subject the paragraph discusses. Sometimes the topic is stated in the first sentence of the paragraph. Sometimes it may be stated in the last sentence. Sometimes the topic is not stated in a sentence, but it can be inferred from reading the paragraph. Read Paragraph 5, and answer the following questions.

1. What is the topic of Paragraph 5?
2. Which two factors mentioned contribute to lower unit costs?
3. How are routing and scheduling simplified?
4. What is done with the finished products at the end of the line?
5. What is a result of each worker having a definite assignment?

H: Topic and development

The purpose of a paragraph is to develop a topic. There are many ways to do this. Sometimes the supporting sentences in the paragraph give more detail or definition to the topic. Sometimes examples are given to illustrate a topic.

Read Paragraph 6 and answer the following questions.

1. What is the topic of Paragraph 6?
2. Is the topic stated in a sentence?
3. List five disadvantages of product layout mentioned in Paragraph 6.

I: Outlining

As you finish reading the passage, fill in the outline below. Begin with Paragraph 4: 4) Product layout: definition; 5) Advantages of product layout; 6) Disadvantages of product layout; 7) Functional layout: definition; 8) Advantages of process layout; 9) Disadvantages of process layout.

Writing

J: Writing a paragraph

Notice that Paragraphs 5, 6, and 7 are comparable to Paragraphs 8, 9, and 10. They are about different topics, but the method of discussion is similar. Noticing the overall structure of a composition, like noticing the structure of a paragraph, will help you to remember the content. We refer to this overall structure of the composition as the organization of the composition.

There are many ways to organize a composition. The organization should contribute to explaining the topic. For example, in this particular passage there is a definition of *layout* followed by a comparison of the two general types of layout. The two comparisons are presented in the last six paragraphs, and the discussions are parallel in organization.

Reread Paragraphs 7 and 9. Notice that certain disadvantages of product layout may sometimes be advantages for process layout. Look at the following outline, which presents four points of comparison. Using this outline, write a paragraph contrasting these two methods of production.

1. Results of Breakdowns
   a. (for product layout) total line shutdown
   b. (for process layout) no total line shutdown
2. Types of Machines
   a. (for product layout) specialized machinery for particular jobs, not easily adapted for other jobs
   b. (for process layout) general type machinery, adaptable to other purposes

3. Volume
   a. (for product layout) high volume of identical products
   b. (for process layout) low volume of varied products
4. Employee Attitude
   a. (for product layout) routine work results in low employee morale
   b. (for process layout) pride of workmanship, high employee morale

K: Writing an organized composition

Supplemental Writing Assignment
Now that you know the advantages and disadvantages of both types of layout, imagine that you were planning the layout for a factory that would produce shoes. Discuss each of the considerations listed below and decide which type of layout to use and why. You may wish to arrange the items in a different order so that the organization of your composition helps you make your points.

In the *introduction* to your composition, begin with a sentence stating that there are several things to consider in planning a shoe factory and write down what they are. In the *body* of the composition discuss each factor in the same order as it was presented in the introduction. In the *conclusion* state why you feel that a specific layout is best.

1. Sizes, styles, colors, variety of products
2. Raw materials
   a. the same for all products?
   b. leather, thread, glues, dyes, nails
3. Steps to production
   a. cutting leather
   b. sewing leather
   c. gluing
   d. hammering nails
   e. other steps
4. Machines needed
5. Volume

Vocabulary Review: Rephrasing

L: Rephrasing words and expressions

Rewrite the following sentences. Substitute expressions from the text for the underlined words, phrases, and clauses.

1. In a well <u>thought out</u> factory layout, everything is <u>set up</u> so that the product and workers <u>proceed</u> in an orderly manner with the <u>greatest efficiency</u>.

2. Proper layout is necessary <u>to prevent products from bunching up at one point on the assembly line</u> and <u>to prevent accumulation</u> of unsold and semi-finished products.

3. A good layout should take the worker into account so that <u>the work place has a pleasant atmosphere</u>.

4. An efficient layout <u>helps workers produce more</u> while <u>controlling costs</u>.

5. Plants and buildings are costly, and the cost <u>is determined by</u> the amount of space involved.

6. With product layout, the factory is <u>designed especially for a certain product</u>.

7. The use of the assembly line lowers the <u>cost for producing one individual item</u>.

8. Raw materials are <u>used up</u> at <u>constant rates</u>.

9. A disadvantage is that if <u>something goes wrong</u> on the assembly line, the entire line is <u>closed down</u>.

10. Finished products roll off the assembly line at one point where it is easy to <u>load them on pallets</u> and <u>send them out on trucks</u>.

Oral Practice

Debate

Resolved: Factory layouts in which each worker is responsible for only one small operation in a production line are generally more cost effective than those in which a worker may be responsible for several operations. (Discuss the arguments for and against this.)

Glossary for Lesson Four
Factory Layout

Adapted: changed to be used for another purpose.

This old railroad car was *adapted* for use as a restaurant.

Alienation: a feeling charaterized by a lack of enthusiasm and interest in one's work.

Workers who perform boring and routine work experience an *alienation* from the products they produce.

Assembly line: a system of machines which enables production to be accomplished by moving the products to the workers so that each worker can complete his part of the assembly.

> Henry Ford was one of the first to use the *assembly line* for the production of automobiles.

Assignment: the post, duty, or task a person or machine is given to perform.

> The inspector's *assignment* is to check the finished products for defects (flaws) in materials or workmanship.

Bottlenecks: places where passage is slowed and products tend to bunch up.

> There is a *bottleneck* today at the end of the assembly line; since one of the forklifts is broken, products cannot be quickly loaded for shipment.

Continuous production: nonstop manufacturing process accomplished by moving the products on an assembly line to the workers and machines.

> *Continuous production* is used in the manufacture of automobiles.

Duplication: the act of doubling or copying; in this lesson, the necessity to double production equipment.

> We can have twice as much production by *duplication* of the present assembly line.

Efficient: using the least amount of energy, time, or labor to produce the most output.

> The most *efficient* way to produce appliances is by using an assembly line.

Equipment: tools and machinery used in production.

> The company has purchased new *equipment* which will help increase production.

Interchangeable: able to be substituted for another part.

> Although these products are manufactured by different companies, they are *interchangeable*.
>
> Radial tires and bias ply tires are not *interchangeable*.

Inventory: stored supplies of raw materials or unsold products.

> We want to slow down production until we can sell some of our *inventory* of finished goods.

Layout: arrangement of personnel, machines, and workspace, etc., in a place of business.

> A good *layout* helps to maximize production and minimize costs.

Maintenance personnel: employees who maintain (service and repair) machinery and buildings.

In order to keep workers from being idle when machines are serviced, we ask our *maintenance personnel* to make repairs at night.

Morale: the mental attitude or feelings of a worker toward his work.

Employee *morale* is very low because we must shut down part of the factory and lay off five hundred workers.

Obsolete: old fashioned, outdated, not useful anymore because technical advances have produced something newer and better.

The automobile made the horse and buggy *obsolete.*

The electric light bulb made kerosene lanterns *obsolete.*

Palletize: to place goods on wooden loading platforms (pallets).

At the end of the assembly line, products are quickly *palletized* and loaded onto trucks.

Plant: factory.

General Motors will build a modern *plant* where cars will be produced by high technology robots.

Product layout: design of a plant and machinery for most efficient production of a particular product.

Product layout is most efficient for mass production of identical items.

Retool: to reset, or replace production machinery to improve or change the product.

The production line is shut down while the company *retools* for next year's models.

Routine: repetitious, uninspired, commonplace, related to an established pattern.

Assembly line work can be very *routine* and boring since the same job is done over and over.

Routing: planning the path that products will travel on the assembly line; planning the way that a person or item will travel as it goes from one point to another.

Because the road was damaged by the storm, we are *routing* traffic onto another road.

Scheduling: planning the time when machines will be in use, workers will be working, or jobs will be done.

The shop foreman is responsible for *scheduling.*

He is *scheduling* this job for next week.

Second shift: a second group of workers who come to work as the first group is leaving.

We doubled production by employing a *second shift* of workers who begin at 4 p.m.

Shutdown: a stopping of the assembly line; a halt in production.

Because of an electrical failure, there was a complete *shutdown* of the line.

Uniform: having exactly the same form or degree; on a bolt or nut, having the same spacing between the threads; having the same shape.

Assembly lines can be used to produce *uniform* products.

These products are of *uniform* size and weight.

Unit cost: the cost of producing one item on the assembly line; it is calculated by dividing total production costs for a certain period by the number of items produced during that period.

We can lower the *unit cost* by using less expensive raw materials.

Introduction to Lesson Five:
Personnel

Both student and businessman are likely to enter into situations where they will need to deal with personnel either as employees or employers. Many of the vocabulary words in this lesson are also useful for a job interview.

It should be remembered that the explanations in the text are for business use, particularly as they relate to personnel. Words such as *staff, vacancy, benefit,* and *retire* have different meanings in other contexts.

The lesson begins with a definition of personnel and its importance to business. The following paragraphs discuss internal and external recruitment, the preparation of the job description, the method of selecting applicants, and the development of personnel policies. Particular attention should be given to the topic of each paragraph.

There is further work with suffixes in the vocabulary exercises. The listening exercise provides the student an opportunity to write a job description, which is good practice in matching a list of specific items with general needs. For additional oral work, students can interview each other for jobs.

Linguistic concepts useful for this lesson include parts of speech, suffixes, and past and present participles used as adjectives.

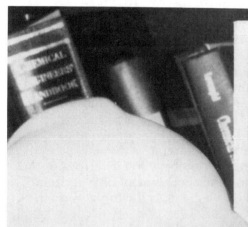

Katy, Gary and André have found professional diversification through BASF Wyandotte's Unique Development Program

Our Technical Personnel Development Program (TPDP) has enabled them to plan and implement their careers according to their individual needs and those of the company.

In our program, you have the opportunity to select job assignments in different departments approximately every six months. Assignments may include operations, engineering, research and development, production, marketing, manufacturing services, technical services, pilot plant work and plant start-ups.

As permanent positions become available which match your individual interests and demonstrated skills, you will be interviewed and may then receive an offer which you alone decide to accept or reject.

In the process, you will gain an "insider's" appreciation of how BASF Wyandotte functions, and the satisfaction of knowing that you have played a significant part in determining the direction of your career.

For complete details, write to: T.G. Karns, Manager, University Relations & Technical Development, BASF Wyandotte Corporation
100 Cherry Hill Road
Parsippany, New Jersey 07054.

An affirmative action employer M/F

5

Personnel

The Importance and Role of the Personnel Department

Paragraph 1

Personnel refers to all the people who work for a firm. Most large
companies have special personnel departments which are responsible
for employer-employee relations. The personnel department is a staff
department, which means that it is not directly involved with production, but that it provides a service to the managers. The most important
services which the personnel department provides are recruiting, that is,
finding new workers or managers for the company, deciding which
applicants are most suitable for employment by the <u>firm</u>, and developing
and <u>implementing</u> personnel policies and procedures for the <u>benefit</u> of
the company as well as the employees.

company
putting into use;
good

Paragraph 2

Most businesses continually need to recruit good personnel to replace
workers who retire or quit and to fill new jobs created when the company

grows; decided on   expands. After management has <u>determined</u> the goals of the company and the positions needed, the personnel department must find qualified people to fill those positions. Depending upon management policy and the nature of the position, recruiting may be done <u>internally</u> or <u>externally</u>. <u>Internal</u> recruitment means that the person <u>chosen for the position is selected from the current employees</u> of the company. This is either by <u>promotion or transfer</u>. <u>Promotion</u> means an employee receives a <u>job with more authority and responsibility than his present job.</u> The employee usually expects to receive an <u>increase in salary</u> along with the new position. A <u>transfer</u> refers to a job or department <u>change for a</u> worker. A transfer without promotion is a <u>lateral transfer.</u> It may involve <u>different working conditions or different hours.</u> Companies that recruit internally often promote internally, which means that the managers have worked their way up from lower positions. It may also mean that the company may hire new employees only at lower positions.

Paragraph 3

External recruitment means that the company is looking for new employees from outside the firm. All companies do some type of external recruitment. If they are looking for employees with special training or education, they will often recruit at university campuses. They make arrangements with the <u>placement office</u> at the campus to interview graduating students. Sometimes they are seeking top level managers who they will recruit from other firms, often from their competitors. Other methods of recruiting involve the use of advertising in newspapers and professional publications, and even paying a fee or <u>commission</u> to an <u>executive placement service.</u>

Paragraph 4

Most recruiting involves a job announcement containing a description of the job. The personnel department produces a formal job description. If the firm is not well known, the job description may begin with some basic information about the company and its products. This is usually followed by the title of the position the company wants to fill, for example, Senior Design Engineer or Vice President in Charge of Finance. Then the duties and responsibilities of the job are given, as well **plan** as where that position fits in the organizational <u>chart</u> (that is, who the person reports to and who the person supervises). Next appear the qualifications for the job, such as the professional training or skills **extra items such** needed. The salary and <u>fringe benefits</u> paid for by the company should **as insurance or** also be mentioned. Finally, the job description will tell the applicant **a retirement fund** exactly what to do if he is interested in the position.

Paragraph 5

person
give

The personnel department should have a method for choosing the best candidate from among the applicants for the position. In some companies this may involve testing prospective employees. Civil service or government jobs often require applicants to compete with each other on written tests. Those applicants with the highest scores are selected for an interview. Other companies may assign points for certain items on the application form, such as experience or education. They may then total the points and select the applicants with the highest totals. After the applications have been evaluated, the best qualified applicants are invited to an interview. In the interview the applicant's personality and ability to work with others may be judged.

Paragraph 6

job

unfavorably

new jobs
complaints

an organization that
looks after the inter-
ests of the workers

Some people feel the most important function of the personnel department is the development of personnel policies. For efficiency and fairness, a company should have a specific formal written procedure for dealing with its employees. Otherwise, decisions must be made on a case by case basis, and this could adversely affect employee morale. These procedures should state working conditions, salary scale, and fringe benefits such as paid vacation, paid sick leave, group insurance, pension or retirement plan—all things received in addition to pay. Part of the policy may also include a procedure for notifying employees of openings or promotional opportunities. In addition, there is often a procedure for handling grievances, which an employee can use if he feels that he has been treated unfairly by the employer. All of these items may be part of a union contract between the employer and the employees who are members of a union.

SAMPLE JOB DESCRIPTION

THE COMPANY:	XYZ Corporation is a leading producer of consumer and industrial cleaning products. XYZ has been supplying these products to the metropolitan area since 1970. XYZ is expanding its production facilities to meet growing customer demand and to enable it to produce for a nationwide market. The philosophy of the company is to encourage employees to make suggestions for the improvement of products and production methods and to reward employees for their contributions. If you would like to be part of this progressive company, please read about the job opportunities listed here.
JOB TITLE:	Production Worker
DUTIES:	Works on line at various tasks involved in production of XYZ products. Reports to line foreman.
EDUCATION AND SKILLS REQUIRED:	High School diploma preferred. Experience in operation of conveyor belt machinery preferred.
HOURS:	Forty hours per week. All shifts available. Days, 8 a.m. to 4 p.m.; Swing, 4 p.m. to midnight; Graveyard, midnight to 8 a.m.
OPPORTUNITY:	Successful performance in this position may lead to promotion to Line Foreman.
WAGES:	$7.00 per hour to start with. Review in three months.
BENEFITS:	Eleven paid holidays; fifteen days paid vacation after one year. One paid sick day per month. Medical and dental insurance available at reduced rates. Employer paid pension plan; profit sharing.
METHOD OF APPLICATION:	Applicants should submit a handwritten application available from the Personnel Department. Pick up applications between 9 a.m. and 5 p.m., Monday through Friday.

SAMPLES OF ITEMS ON A JOB APPLICATION

APPLICATION FOR EMPLOYMENT

NORTHROP UNIVERSITY

INGLEWOOD, CALIFORNIA 90306
(213) 776-3410 or 641-3470

An Equal Opportunity Employer

EQUAL AND FAIR CONSIDERATION SHALL BE GIVEN TO EVERY APPLICANT FOR EMPLOYMENT. SELECTION OF EMPLOYEES WILL BE BASED UPON THE QUALIFICATIONS AND EXPERIENCE OF THE INDIVIDUAL FOR THE JOB.

To our applicants: Please answer all questions completely. The more we know about your qualifications, abilities and experience, the better we will be able to offer you positions suitable to you. If you need help to complete this application, please request assistance from a member of this office. We will be pleased to serve you.

Name _____ Today's date _____
      Last   First   Middle Initial

Present address _____
      No.   Street   City   State   Zip

Tel. No. _____ How long have you lived at above address? _____ Social Security No. _____

How long did you
Previous address _____ live there? _____
      No.   Street   City   State   Zip

Can you, after employment, provide proof of U.S. citizenship, <u>or</u> a current valid visa which would permit you to work in this country? _____

Person to be notified in case of
accident or emergency _____
      Name

_____
      Address   Telephone No.

Have you ever been convicted of a crime (excluding traffic violations)? If "yes" describe in full, including disposition (a conviction record will not necessarily bar you from employment here) _____

_____

_____

A typical application for employment form.

Position(s) applied for _____ Rate of pay expected $ _____ per ____

If your application is considered favorably, on what date will you be available for work? _____

How or by whom were you referred to Northrop University? _____

Specific days and hours
Would you work full-time? _____ part-time? _____ if part-time: _____

Were you previously employed by us? _____ If "yes," when? _____

KNOWLEDGE/SKILLS/ABILITIES

School Attended	Name and Location	Last Year Completed				Course of Study
Jr. High School	Name: City: State:		7	8	9	
High School	Name: City: State:		10	11	12	
Jr. College	Name: City: State:		1	2		
College or University	Name: City: State:	1	2	3	4	
Graduate School	Name: City: State:	1	2	3	4	
Other (Include Trade School)	Name: City: State:					

Describe knowledge, skills, or abilities gained in your studies which relate to the job(s) for which you are applying:

_____

_____

_____

List any knowledge, skills or abilities obtained through on-the-job training or employment that you feel may be used in your employment here:

_____

_____

List any present courses of study, training, hobbies or activities which relate to the job(s) for which you are applying:

_____

_____

_____

List any knowledge, skills or abilities obtained doing volunteer work, or household duties: _____

_____

_____

Typing speed: Manual _____ Electric _____ Executive _____ Shorthand speed _____

Office machines operated: _____

_____

EMPLOYMENT/EXPERIENCE

Please list all jobs and activities for the past **ten years** or since attending school as a full-time student. Include part-time employment and self-employment. Include experience gained doing volunteer work or community service work. **List the most recent employment and activities first.**

NAME OF EMPLOYER				YOUR JOB TITLE
ADDRESS OF EMPLOYER				DESCRIBE WORK YOU PERFORMED
CITY		STATE		
SUPERVISOR'S NAME AND JOB TITLE				
DATE STARTED	DATE ENDED	DURATION yr. mo.	PAY	REASON FOR LEAVING

NAME OF EMPLOYER	YOUR JOB TITLE			

ADDRESS OF EMPLOYER	DESCRIBE WORK YOU PERFORMED

CITY	STATE	

SUPERVISOR'S NAME AND JOB TITLE	HOURS PER WEEK

DATE STARTED	DATE ENDED	DURATION yr. mo.	PAY	REASON FOR LEAVING

NAME OF EMPLOYER	YOUR JOB TITLE

ADDRESS OF EMPLOYER	DESCRIBE WORK YOU PERFORMED

CITY	STATE	

SUPERVISOR'S NAME AND JOB TITLE	

DATE STARTED	DATE ENDED	DURATION yr. mo.	PAY	REASON FOR LEAVING –

NAME OF EMPLOYER	YOUR JOB TITLE

ADDRESS OF EMPLOYER	DESCRIBE WORK YOU PERFORMED

CITY	STATE	

SUPERVISOR'S NAME AND JOB TITLE	

DATE STARTED	DATE ENDED	DURATION yr. mo.	PAY	REASON FOR LEAVING

NAME OF EMPLOYER	YOUR JOB TITLE

ADDRESS OF EMPLOYER	DESCRIBE WORK YOU PERFORMED

CITY	STATE	

SUPERVISOR'S NAME AND JOB TITLE				
DATE STARTED	DATE ENDED	DURATION yr. mo.	PAY	REASON FOR LEAVING

ORGANIZATIONAL CHART FOR A CORPORATION

Board of Directors

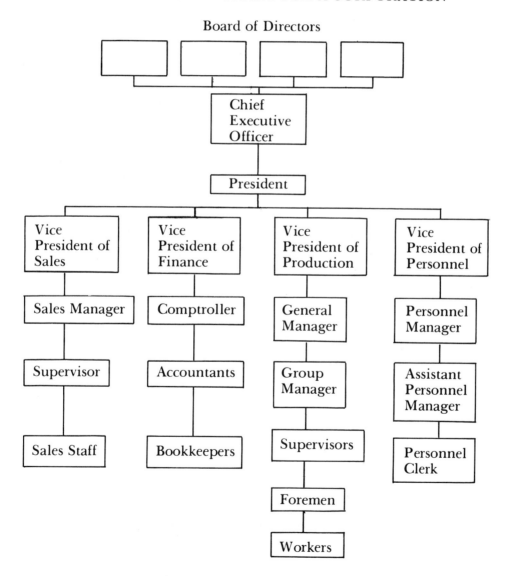

Vocabulary Building Introduction

A: Vocabulary in context

Determining meanings from context
The following sentences indicate the meaning of the underlined word or words directly as in a definition or indirectly by means of another element in the sentence. Read the following sentences and try to understand the underlined words from the context.

1. Anyone who works for a company is part of the personnel of that company.
2. A staff department is a department of a company that provides a service to the managers. A staff department is not directly involved with production.
3. Recruiting refers to finding new employees or managers for the company.
4. When workers retire or quit, the personnel department must recruit new workers to fill the vacancies.
5. A company recruits internally if it wishes to fill vacancies by transferring or promoting current employees.
6. External recruitment means that a company is seeking new employees from outside the firm.
7. When an employee is promoted, he receives a position with more authority and responsibility and usually an increase in salary.
8. The worker was transferred from one department to the other.
9. Fringe benefits include paid vacation, medical insurance, and employer contributions to a pension plan. Fringe benefits are what the employee receives in addition to his wages.
10. There is a grievance procedure for handling complaints when an employee feels he has been treated unfairly.

B: Matching

Match the words on the left with the expressions on the right.

1. promote   _____ a. complaint of unfair treatment

2. vacancy   _____ b. paid sick leave, for example

3. retire   _____ c. job opening

4. external   _____ d. seeking new employees

5. recruitment _____ e. accounting, for example

6. fringe benefits   ————— f . outside

7. grievance   ————— g. to assign a more important job

8. staff departments ————— h. to stop working after a certain age

C: Parts of speech

The root of the word is the basic part of the word. It carries the primary meaning. The suffix is an ending attached to the word which usually indicates its grammatical use, that is, whether it is a noun, verb, adjective, or adverb. The following groups of words are all related in meaning because they have the same roots. Notice the different suffixes indicating different parts of speech.

Verb	*Noun*	*Adjective*
qualify	qualification	qualified
promote	promotion	promotional
employ	employer, employee, employment	employable
determine	determination	determining
apply	application, applicant	applicable
authorize	authority	authorized
describe	description	descriptive
base	basis	basic
compete	competitor, competition	competing
recruit	recruit, recruitment	
staff	staff	staff
require	requirement	required

Analyze the following sentences to determine the part of speech of the missing words. Supply the correct form of the word.

authorize   **1.** His new job has more ————————————and

responsibility. He is now ———————————

to sign checks.

applicant   **2.** People who wish to ——————————— for

the position should fill out an ———————————

for the personnel department. ———————————

chosen for interviews will be notified by mail.

promote

3. The personnel department is giving a _____ examination to see which of the current employees will be _____ to the new position.

descriptive

4. The job _____ states the job title. It also _____ all the duties as well as the requirements for employment.

basic

5. The interviewer will _____ his decision on the applicant's personality and qualifications.

competitor

6. They hired the new manager from a _____ company.

determine

7. A _____ will be made based on the experience of the applicants.

require

8. Does the applicant have the _____ skills? Does he meet all the other _____?

qualification

9. Are you _____ for this job? Fill out an application. _____ applicants will be contacted for an interview.

recruit

10. This company has a policy of internal _____. We always try to fill managerial positions with current employees.

Listening and Note-Taking Skills

D: Outlining

Listen to Paragraphs 2 and 3 and write an outline of them.

E: Listing specific information from a narrative

A job description is usually written as a list, not as a paragraph. Listen to Paragraph 4, which explains what a job description is. Think of a specific job, then make a list of the items you would include in the job description.

Reading Comprehension

The following exercises are designed to increase vocabulary and reading comprehension.

F: Completion

Select the answer which best completes the meaning of the sentence.

1. The personnel department must decide which applicants are the most suitable for

   a. benefits.   c. employee.
   b. employment.   d. promotion.

2. To fill the vacancy in the accounting department, they are seeking the person who is best

   a. promoted.   c. qualified.
   b. competitive.   d. authorized.

3. The person being promoted receives more

   a. authority.   c. salary.
   b. responsibility. d. all of these.

4. Companies which recruit internally hire new workers

   a. at all levels.   c. at beginning levels.
   b. at the manage- d. all of these.
      rial level.

5. If a company is recruiting new employees, they might

   a. advertise in   c. qualify for the job.
      newspapers.
   b. promote a new d. none of these.
      employee.

6. The job description tells about a job opening at a company. It would most likely state

   a. the supervisor's c. what the applicant looks like.
      name.
   b. the duties and   d. the applicant's name.
      responsibilities.

7. As personnel director, he is authorized to issue employee identification. Issuing employee identification is one of his

   a. authorities.   c. qualifications.
   b. requirements. d. responsibilities.

8. The personnel policies should provide a method for settling employee grievances. An employee who has a grievance

   a. may be promoted. c. should fill out an application.
   b. will be fired.   d. thinks he was treated unfairly.

9. The committee will base their decision on the applicant's qualifications. This means they will decide whom to

  a. apply.   c. authorize.
  b. qualify.   d. hire.

10. The personnel department announces a promotional examination next week. This examination is intended for

  a. supervisors.   c. current employees.
  b. new recruits.   d. competitors.

G: Comprehension questions

Study the following questions about Paragraphs 5 and 6. Then read the passage and answer the questions. Write complete sentences and use your own words. Do not copy sentences from the passage.

1. What two methods do employers use to select applicants for an interview?
2. What can interviews reveal about the applicants?
3. What is a *prospective* employee?
4. Besides recruiting and choosing new workers, what is another important function of the personnel department?
5. Why does a company need to have a policy which is written down? What could be the result of not having an established policy?
6. What are fringe benefits?
7. Under what conditions are there grievances?
8. According to the article, what is one function of a union?

Writing

H: Writing general and specific paragraphs

Using your list from Exercise F, write a paragraph describing the company, followed by a job description.

Vocabulary Review: Rephrasing

I: Rephrasing words

Rewrite the following sentences. Replace the words in italics with expressions from the text which have the same meaning.

1. The personnel department is a *service* department.
2. Businesses continually need to *find* good personnel to take the place of workers who *quit because of old age.*
3. If they are looking for managers, they might recruit from *another company in the same business.*
4. Often there is a policy for handling *complaints about treatment.*
5. Because of his accomplishments, he received a *job with more authority and responsibility.*
6. He was selected for the job because he had the best *skills and abilities.*
7. The policies describe *what employees receive in addition to salary.*
8. The *job seekers* with the highest scores will be selected for an interview.
9. This company *looks for workers from outside the company.*
10. He *changed jobs* from the accounting department to the personnel department.

Job Interview

The following is a sample job interview. After acting this dialogue out in class engage in similar interviews applying for other jobs.

INTERVIEWER: We are looking for an executive secretary who has excellent skills as well as good organizational ability. Tell me about your qualifications.

APPLICANT: I can take shorthand at 120 words a minute and type 90 words a minute. I have also had experience using Wang and IBM word processing equipment. At my last job I reorganized the filing system, planned my boss's travel itinerary, and organized and planned the agenda for the board of directors' meeting.

INTERVIEWER: In this job you would also need to answer routine correspondence and telephone inquiries. Have you had any experience in these areas?

APPLICANT: When I worked as an appointments secretary, I had to screen my boss's phone calls and mail, as well as attend to routine matters. It was my responsibility to decide which matters were important and which were trivial.

INTERVIEWER: Do you have any questions about the position?

APPLICANT: Yes. I would like to know what the possibilities for advancement are within this company.

INTERVIEWER: Although this is the top secretarial position within the organization, there are regular salary increments based on the amount of time an employee has served the company, and you can look forward to generous pay increases if you remain with us. Generally, employees are reviewed once a year by their superiors and decisions about raises are made at that time.

Glossary for Lesson Five
Personnel

Applicant: a person who is seeking a job and has taken some specific action to get the job.

All *applicants* for the position should have a minimum of two years' experience.

Competitor: another individual or firm in a similar business that tries to attract the same customers or clients.

Coca Cola and Pepsi Cola are *competitors* in the soft drink business.

Duty: the obligation or responsibility of a job.

The policeman has the *duty* to protect the citizens.

Employee: a person who works for another, usually for pay.

General Motors Corporation has several thousand *employees*. The company provides generous benefits for the *employees*.

Employer: a person or company that provides work.

The *employer* must pay social security taxes for each worker.

The *employer* provides medical insurance for the workers.

Evaluate: to decide the value or worth of something; to measure an applicant's qualifications.

People who apply for the job will be *evaluated* regarding their experience and skills.

Expand: to grow, to add space or employees to a company.

Because our company has *expanded*, there will be a need for new employees.

Experience: ability acquired through practice of a skill, craft, or job.

The applicant has five years' *experience* as an electrician.

Fringe benefit: what is received in addition to salary.

This company provides generous *fringe benefits* for its employees, including insurance, a pension plan, and medical and dental payments.

Goals: purposes, what a company wants to accomplish.

It is our *goal* this year to increase sales by ten percent.

Grievance: a reason to complain about treatment or an injustice.

The employee who was fired filed a *grievance* with the personnel department.

Implement: to put into effect.

The new personnel policy will be *implemented* July 1.

Interview: a face to face meeting and question and answer session with the person who makes hiring decisions.

Applicants will have an *interview* with the personnel director.

Lateral: from one side to another; on the organizational chart, across rather than up.

She was secretary to the sales manager, but now she is secretary to the production manager. She didn't receive a promotion, just a *lateral* transfer.

Manager: a person who directs, supervises, or controls a business or department of a business.

The sales *manager* has hired three new salesmen.

The *manager* can decide who will receive the promotion.

Organizational chart: a schematic drawing showing the relationships between managers, supervisors, and workers.

According to the *organizational chart,* the Vice President for Finance supervises the Accounting Department.

Personnel: all the people who work for a company.

This parking lot is reserved for company *personnel.*

We could increase production if we had enough *personnel.*

Contact the *personnel* department to apply for a job.

Promotion: change of jobs to one with more authority and responsibility, and usually an increase in salary.

He was a salesman, but he received a *promotion* and now he is the sales manager.

Qualify: have the necessary abilities and skills for a job.

A person can *qualify* for a government job on the basis of his score on the civil service examination.

Recruit: to find new workers for a company or a position.

The personnel department needs to *recruit* some new secretaries.

Responsibility: liability, accountability, situation of having to explain one's own actions and answer for them.

The manager has the *responsibility* to see that all the work is completed by Friday.

Salary: amount of money paid regularly for work.

As an accountant for our company, you will earn a *salary* of $40,000 per year.

Staff: the employees responsible for internal operation of the organization rather than production.

The Accounting Department is a *staff* department.

Suitable: able to be used for a specific purpose.

As soon as we find a *suitable* applicant, we will hire him.

This new typewriter is *suitable* for home or office use.

Training: a program of learning a specific skill.

New employees are given three weeks' *training* in the operation of the machinery.

Transfer: a change of jobs from one division of a company to another without an increase in responsibility, authority, or salary.

He received a *transfer* from the personnel department to the advertising department.

Introduction to Lesson Six:
Marketing

Marketing is an aspect of business that has worldwide importance. This chapter deals with the changing notions of marketing and how marketing relates to all aspects of any business.

Beginning with this lesson, there is a shift in emphasis from the more technical aspects of business discussed earlier to a concern with the theoretical and planning aspects. The market is not merely a location for buying and selling products; it is also a concept influencing many other business decisions. Paralleling the shift in emphasis in the material is a shift in approach as well.

In this lesson there is more emphasis on understanding similar ideas and similar concepts rather than simply understanding the similarity in meaning between two words. The first vocabulary exercise, for example, requires the student to find a *sentence* which expresses the same meaning as another, rather than merely a synonymous word. The reading comprehension passages also require the student to think analytically, make inferences, and use logic.

Linguistic concepts useful for this lesson include complex sentences expressing conditions and cause and effect, transitional elements, sentence adverbs, and adverbial phrases.

Marketing includes designing products for specific purposes. This Mack truck has been designed to transport coal from the point where it is mined to a point where it is loaded on a train.

6

Marketing

The Changing Concept of Marketing

Paragraph 1

The terms *market* and *marketing* can have several meanings depending upon how they are used. The term *stock market* refers to the buying and selling of shares in corporations as well as other activities related to stock trading and pricing. The important world stock markets are in London, Geneva, New York, Tokyo, and Singapore. Another type of market is a grocery market, which is a place where people purchase food. When economists use the word *market* they mean a set of forces or conditions that determine the price of a product, such as the supply available for sale and the demand for it by consumers. The term *marketing* in business includes all of these meanings, and more.

Paragraph 2

idea In the past, the <u>concept</u> of marketing emphasized sales. The producer or manufacturer made a product he wanted to sell. Marketing was the task of figuring out how to sell the product. Basically, selling the product would be accomplished by sales promotion, which included advertising and personal selling. In addition to sales promotion, marketing also involved the physical distribution of the product to the places where it was actually sold. Distribution consisted of transportation, storage, and related services such as financing, standardization and grading, and the related risks.

Paragraph 3

includes
believes

The modern marketing concept encompasses all of the activities mentioned, but it is based on a different set of principles. It subscribes to the notion that production can be economically justified only by consumption. In other words, goods should be produced only if they can be sold. Therefore, the producer should consider who is going to buy the product—or what the *market* for the product is—before production begins. This is very different from making a product and then thinking about how to sell it.

Paragraph 4

only

before

Marketing now involves first deciding what the customer wants, and designing and producing a product that satisfies these wants at a profit to the company. Instead of concentrating solely on production, the company must consider the desires of the consumer, and this is much more difficult since it involves human behavior. Production, on the other hand, is mostly an engineering problem. Thus, demand and market forces are still an important aspect of modern marketing, but they are considered prior to the production process.

Paragraph 5

Because products are often marketed internationally, distribution has increased in importance. Goods must be at the place where the customer needs them or brought there. This is known as place utility; it adds value to a product. However, many markets are separated from the place of production, which means that often both raw materials and finished products must be transported to the points where they are needed.

Paragraph 6

in great volumes

goods

Raw materials requiring little or no special treatment can be transported by rail, ship, or barge at low cost. Large quantities of raw materials travel as bulk freight, but finished products that often require special treatment, such as refrigeration or careful handling, are usually transported by truck. This merchandise freight is usually smaller in volume and requires quicker delivery. *Merchandise freight* is a term for the transportation of manufactured goods.

Paragraph 7

paid for with loans or other sources of money

Along all points of the distribution channel various amounts of storage are required. The time and manner of such storage depends upon the type of product. Inventories of this stored merchandise often need to be <u>financed</u>.

Paragraph 8

Modern marketing is therefore a coordinated system of many business activities, but basically it involves four things: (1) selling the correct product at the proper place, (2) selling it at a price determined by demand, (3) satisfying a customer's need and wants, and (4) producing a profit for the company.

Vocabulary Building Introduction

A: Rephrasing ideas

Find sentences from the text which have the same meaning or express the same general idea as the sentences below.

1. Shares of stock are traded on the stock exchange where market forces determine the price.
2. The grocery market is the location where the buying and selling of food takes place.
3. Economists believe that if many people desire a product which is not available in great quantities, the price will increase.
4. In the past the most important function of marketing was sales.
5. Marketing used to be the job of thinking about how to sell the product.
6. People will buy a product if it is promoted by salesmen and if the company advertises it.
7. Part of marketing is delivering the merchandise to the stores where people shop for it.
8. Food products are classified into groups according to their size and quality. Eggs and meat are graded according to government standards.

9. Modern marketing includes many activities, but it is based on a different concept.

10. Modern marketing is based on the idea that goods cannot be produced for profit unless someone will buy them.

B: Matching

Match the words below with the definitions indicated in exercise A.

1. stock exchange   ————————   a. consider most important

2. market forces   ————————   b. distribution

3. desire   ————————   c. methods to increase sales, like advertising

4. delivering   ————————   d. amount available for sale

5. concept   ————————   e. supply and demand

6. consumers   ————————   f. place to buy and sell shares of corporations

7. promotion   ————————   g. notion

8. consumption   ————————   h. purchase

9. supply   ————————   i. customers

10. emphasize   ————————   j. demand

Listening and Note-Taking Skills

C: Form and content clues

The material in this lesson is basically a definition or explanation of the term *marketing*. In order to understand the lesson, therefore, it is necessary to understand the manner in which the terms are defined and explained. There are certain words in the text which indicate the order and method of the explanation. There are other words which actually do the explaining and defining. Look at the words listed below. They are taken from the first four paragraphs. Some of them indicate the *form* of the definition while others indicate the *content*. Adverbs of time and limiting adjectives generally indicate the form or method. Verbs and phrases generally indicate content or meaning.

Study the following terms and decide whether they indicate the arrangement of ideas or the meaning of ideas. The terms are listed in the same order as in the paragraph.

Paragraph 1	Paragraph 2	Paragraph 3	Paragraph 4
several	in the past	encompasses	now
refers to	emphasized	but	involves
other	task of	different	first
related to	accomplished by	notion that	solely
another	included	in other words	on the other hand
indicates	in addition	therefore	thus
when	involved		
mean	consists of		
determine	such as		
such as	and		
and			
includes			

D: Comprehension questions

Now listen to Paragraphs 1 through 4. The word list in Exercise C should help you understand the order of the material and the content. The following questions can be answered in order as you listen to the text.

1. In Paragraph 1 there are examples of three types of markets. What are they?
2. In general, what is said about the term *marketing*?
3. In Paragraph 2 the author mentions two aspects of marketing. What are they?
4. What are two activities of sales promotion the author mentions in the second paragraph?
5. What are three aspects of distribution?
6. Give three examples of related services.
7. How does the beginning of Paragraph 3 contrast with the first sentence in Paragraph 2?
8. How does modern marketing differ from the past ideas and practices of marketing?
9. According to Paragraph 4, what effect does the theory of modern marketing have on production decisions?
10. What makes solving marketing problems more difficult than solving production problems?

E: Outlining

Listen to Paragraphs 1 through 4 again and make an outline of them that includes the following major headings: I. Market and Marketing; II. Marketing in the Past; III. Modern Marketing; IV. The Method of Modern Marketing.

F: Analytic questions

This lesson is organized in two parts. The first part traces the development of the marketing concept historically, beginning with the basic idea of buying and selling and concluding with a theoretical consideration of how marketing should influence production. The second part (Paragraphs 5, 6, and 7) discusses the practical side of traditional marketing activities of distribution and related services.

To formulate a clear and concise definition that encompasses all aspects of a problem, it is often necessary to examine many examples. This is true for many fields of activity. For example, a judge can reach a decision only after he has considered all the facts. The solution to a problem can be found only after thorough analysis.

Answer the following questions about Paragraphs 5, 6, 7, and 8.

1. What activity of marketing deals with the need for goods to be at the place where customers can use them?
2. How does distribution add to the value of the product?
3. List three characteristics of bulk freight transport.
4. What type of freight is best suited for bulk transport? Give specific examples.
5. How does the cost of rail freight compare with truck freight?
6. What conclusions can you draw about the speed of various forms of transport?
7. Why do you think finished products require faster transport than raw materials?
8. Is financing more important for finished products than for raw materials? Why?
9. Why does the author conclude that marketing is a coordinated system of activities?

Reading Comprehension

G: Multiple choice

This exercise is designed to increase vocabulary and reading comprehension. Select the answer which best completes the meaning of the sentence.

1. In the past the main objective of marketing was sales promotion. Marketers were people who

    a. bought and sold stock.   c. tried to sell products.
    b. consumed.   d. supplied and demanded.

2. The word *market* can have several meanings. A person who wants to buy food uses the word to indicate

   a. standardization and grading.   c. sales prices.
   b. a place where groceries are   d. supply and demand.
      for sale.

3. Modern marketing aims to satisfy the wants of the consumer. Marketing personnel should consider first of all

   a. how to advertise the product.   c. how to distribute the product.
   b. what products the customer   d. engineering problems.
      desires.

4. Marketing is an important consideration for

   a. the consumer.   c. all aspects of production.
   b. the distributor.   d. the salesman.

5. Raw materials can be transported in bulk at low cost. Finished goods which sometimes require special treatment usually are shipped by truck. Transportation by truck is probably

   a. what the customer wants.   c. slow.
   b. the best marketing method.   d. more expensive.

6. Demand and market forces are considered prior to production. Before designing and producing the product, companies consider

   a. the supply of consumers.   c. distribution to the consumers.
   b. the desire by consumers to   d. all the marketing activities.
      purchase a product.

7. Between the producer and the consumer certain goods are stored along the way because there may be great distances between the point of production and the point of sale. Storing along the distribution channel

   a. is suitable for all products.   c. makes standardization and
                                          grading necessary.
   b. makes quicker delivery to   d. does not add to the cost of
      consumers.   the product.

8. Economists use the word *market* to refer to a set of forces or conditions which determine the price of a product. This particular meaning of the word *market*

   a. is not important for people   c. has no effect on the stock
      who are not economists.   market.
   b. describes in general how   d. considers only demand, but
      prices are determined   not supply.

9. Among other things, modern marketing considers selling the correct product at the proper place. This means that

   a. place utility and consumer demand must be considered.
   b. advertising will help increase sales.
   c. distribution is more important than product design.
   d. if a product is for sale, someone will buy it.

10. Modern marketing is a coordinated system of business activities because

   a. it involves solving design problems to meet consumer demands.
   b. it involves having the product at the right place at the right time.
   c. it considers the profitability of the company.
   d. all of the above.

Writing

H: Writing a paragraph

The economist's idea of a market is more general than either of the other two interpretations of market in Paragraph 1. Write a paragraph stating how the idea of market can be applied to sales promotion and distribution. You can begin by stating that the two most important market forces are supply and demand. Explain how sales promotion is probably a response to supply, and distribution to demand. Try to conclude with a general statement about how business enterprise reacts to these two forces.

Vocabulary Review: Rephrasing

I: Rephrasing words and expressions

Rewrite the following sentences. Replace the words and expressions in *italics* with expressions from the text which have the same meaning.

1. When economists use the word "market," they mean conditions which *set* the price of a product, for example, the *amount* of product available for sale and the *desire* for the product on the part of *customers*.

2. In the past the concept of marketing *considered selling most important*.

3. Marketing used to be the *activity of determining* how to sell the product.

4. Marketing also involved the *transportation* of the product to places where it was actually sold.

5. Distribution consists of transportation, *warehousing*, and related services such as *providing credit* and *ensuring uniformity of size and quality.*

6. The modern marketing concept *includes* all of the activities mentioned above.

7. It *believes* that production can be economically justified only *through sales to willing buyers.*

8. Marketing now involves first *determining* what the customer wants, and then *planning* and producing a product to *fulfill* those wants.

9. Many markets are *a great distance* from the place of production.

10. *A shipment of finished products* is usually *less bulky* and requires quicker delivery.

Oral Practice

Debate

Resolved: It is more important to have your product available in as many locations as possible than to try to determine exactly those locations where you know there will be customers for it. (Discuss the arguments for and against this.)

Glossary for Lesson Six
Marketing

Advertising: the use of paid commercial messages for the purpose of selling products or ideas.

Advertising can help to increase sales.

Barge: a large boat usually with a flat bottom used for transporting goods on inland waterways.

Coal and iron ore are transported on *barges.*

Consumer: a person or company who buys a product for his own use.

When the price of oil increases, *consumers* pay more for gasoline.

Consumption: the act of buying products for one's own use.

Because of cold winter weather, the *consumption* of heating oil has increased.

Coordinated: acting in common and in harmony with another's movements.

Modern marketing is a *coordinated* system of many business activities.

The rate of production should be *coordinated* to the rate of consumption.

Demand: the desire on the part of consumers for a product or service.

The *demand* for small cars has increased due to the increase in fuel prices.

Designing: planning and arranging a product with a specific purpose in mind.

They are busy *designing* a new computer for the banking industry.

Desires: wants; products consumers need or would like to buy.

Several different types of automobiles are available to satisfy the *desires* and needs of the marketplace.

Determine: to fix or to establish in a free market.

The price of a product will be *determined* by the quantity available for sale and the desire of the consumer.

Distribution: transportation of the product from the point of production to various points where it can be sold.

Modern transportation capabilities make possible worldwide *distribution* of Japanese, American, and German products.

Distribution channel or channel of distribution: route or pathway of a product from manufacturer to ultimate consumer.

Products such as cigarettes, candy, and soft drinks, which are available for sale in many locations, move through a more complex *distribution channel* than products such as automobiles, which are usually available only at certain dealers.

Emphasize: consider most important.

Advertisers *emphasize* the name of their product as well as the benefits consumers get from purchasing and using it.

Finance: acquire capital for, extend credit for.

An automobile dealer has many cars for sale on his lot. Unless he has enough money to pay the manufacturer for them, he must arrange to borrow the money to *finance* his inventory.

Grading: establishing the quality of a product by comparing it to a certain standard.

Grading is most important for agricultural products.

The highest quality eggs and milk are *graded* AA.

The government has established standards for *grading* tires.

Inventories: stores of unsold goods; supplies on hand.

Oil companies like to keep *inventories* at a ninety day supply.

Continuous production requires adequate *inventories* of raw materials.

Market: a group of buyers for whom a product is produced.

There is a worldwide *market* for American agricultural products.

Market forces: various conditions and situations such as supply and demand which determine price.

Because *market forces* are favorable, we can probably increase the price without suffering a decrease in sales volume.

Marketing: that area of business concerned with producing and selling the right product so that the company will make a profit.

In the design of new products, *marketing* considerations should be considered.

Personal selling: the activity of personally helping and convincing prospective buyers to purchase an idea, product, or service.

Automobiles and real estate are products which require *personal selling*. Advertising is not enough.

Place utility: the increase in value of a product due to its availability at a certain place or time.

In an area with no roads, a pair of good walking shoes may have more *place utility* than an automobile.

Principle: a basic rule.

Modern marketing is based on the *principle* that production can be economically justified only by consumption.

Production: the act of making goods and services.

The *production* of steel will increase to meet the demands of the market.

Sales promotion: business activities with the goal of increasing sales of the product.

Advertising and price reductions are examples of *sales promotion*.

Standardization: making products of uniform size and specifications so that the characteristics of a product can be determined from a description rather than from examination.

Mass production is possible only because of *standardization* of parts.

Because of *standardization*, 35 mm film manufactured in Germany will fit a 35 mm camera produced in Japan.

Stock market: a place where shares of corporations and other securities are bought and sold.

The New York Stock Exchange is one of the world's most important *stock markets.*

Supply: the amount of a product available for sale.

Because of poor weather, the harvest was bad and the world *supply* of grain is less than last year.

Task: duty or job.

Marketing used to be the *task* of trying to sell already manufactured products.

Transportation: movement of products from the place of manufacture to the place of sale.

Air *transportation* is generally more expensive than truck *transportation,* but by using air freight, a company can often eliminate the need for several warehouses.

Introduction to Lesson Seven: Distribution

Distribution is a major business activity because virtually everyone from the producer to the consumer is involved in it. This lesson deals with the steps involved in distribution.

The overall organization of the lesson consists of a definition followed by a discussion of the three areas that determine the type of distribution. Like the previous lesson, this one requires the student to focus on certain concepts and ideas rather than on definitions. These concepts involve the nature of the product, the manufacturer's plans for marketing, and the consumer's perception of the product. All three of these factors interrelate to determine the point of sale and the method of distribution.

The reading exercises focus on the way details explain and develop main ideas. The writing exercises require students to develop the main ideas as they consider problems involved with the distribution of particular products.

Linguistic concepts useful for this lesson are appositives, noun phrases and clauses, coordinating conjunctions, and parallel structures.

The *Wall Street Journal* is distributed to local printing facilities world-wide using an electronic channel of distribution. Time and costs for transportation are virtually eliminated.

7

Distribution

Methods and Routes of Distribution

Paragraph 1

After a product has been manufactured, the next step is to find out which methods and routes should be used to bring it to market. This involves <u>channels</u> of distribution.

methods

Paragraph 2

person who purchases it for his own use; when a product may be sold directly to a consumer

title

The channel of distribution or trade channel refers to the route the product takes on the way from the manufacturer or producer to the <u>ultimate consumer</u>. The simplest form of distribution is <u>direct sale</u>. For example, a grower sells produce directly to a customer at a roadside stand. However, most often the channel of distribution involves middlemen. Middlemen are people who take possession of merchandise and take title to it or arrange for transfer of <u>ownership</u>. The reason middlemen are needed is that a particular customer or consumer desires many products, which come from many manufacturers, and it is impossible for the consumer to purchase every product from the producer. For example, in offices, pencils, paper, desks, chairs, lamps, cabinets, and many other products are used. Each of these products may be manufactured in a different part of the country. The office purchasing agent needs to be able to purchase different quantities of these items at one place that is convenient for him.

Paragraph 3

The job of the middleman is to collect the different products from the various manufacturers, and then to divide them into amounts which the customers require. The middleman gives the products place utility by delivering or transporting them to where they are needed. Two types of middlemen are merchant middlemen, who actually take title to the merchandise, and agent middlemen, who arrange for the transfer of title between manufacturer and wholesaler. An example of a merchant middleman might be a person who owns a warehouse, buys large quantities of goods from manufacturers, and then distributes them to companies who purchase smaller quantities. An example of an agent middleman would be a broker who earns a commission by putting buyer and seller in contact with one another.

Paragraph 4

The channel of distribution selected for consumer products sold on the retail market depends upon the type of product. Some items are considered convenience goods. They are generally products which have a low price and can be found at several convenient locations. Examples are chewing gum, cigarettes, and soft drinks. One generally goes to the closest place to buy these kinds of products. In this case, convenience is more important than price. The customer is willing to pay for place utility. Convenience goods are found at supermarkets, convenience stores, and even in vending machines. These goods must be widely distributed. They may, therefore, go through several middlemen before they arrive at the place where the consumer purchases them.

Paragraph 5

Other consumer products are classified as shopping goods. These are products which generally cost more than convenience goods and require more consideration of price and quality than do convenience goods. A customer shopping for a television set or other major home appliance would probably consider several different products and shop at several different locations to compare quality and price before making a decision about a purchase.

Paragraph 6

stores
help
Shopping goods can be found at various retail <u>outlets</u>. A full service retail store is one where sales staff <u>wait on</u> customers and can explain to them the various aspects and features of the product. The product is generally on display. The cost of space and the sales and commission are added to the cost of the product.

Paragraph 7

Discount houses are another type of retail outlet. Products are offered for sale at a lower price because there is a small sales staff or the retailer has been able to reduce overhead in another manner. For example, the store could be in a warehouse or some place where rents are lower.

sells; large amounts
styles
Discount houses usually carry only merchandise that <u>moves</u> in <u>high volume</u>. They may not have the large selection of brands and <u>lines</u> available at a full service store. Sometimes they can receive discounts from wholesalers by purchasing in quantity or by purchasing discontinued models, and sometimes they can deal directly with manufacturers, eliminating the middleman.

Paragraph 8

Two of the larger types of retail distributors are franchise stores and chain stores. A franchise store is a store that is independently owned, but

larger
buyer of the
franchise
operates under a franchise or license from a <u>parent</u> company. The <u>franchisee</u> pays a fee for the license and a certain percentage of the total sales to the parent company. In return for this, the parent company supplies the products and promotes sales through advertising. Franchise stores are particularly popular in the fast food industry. McDonald's and Kentucky Fried Chicken have franchises worldwide. Franchise stores and chain stores are similar in the ways they are run and the fact that the same merchandise is generally carried throughout the chain or franchise. The main difference between a chain store and a franchise store is that the chain store is owned by the parent company. Some supermarkets, such as Safeway, are operated as chain stores. Department stores such as Sears are also chain stores. The advantage that franchise stores and chain stores enjoy in distribution is that they are often vertically integrated. This means the parent company controls the warehouses, the trucking lines, and sometimes the manufacture of the product. Vertical integration should allow a parent company to control costs and maximize profits. However, sometimes vertically integrated organizations become so large that they actually cost more to operate. A large expensive bureaucracy is needed to run a large organization.

Vocabulary Building Introduction

A: Rephrasing ideas

Find sentences from the text which have the same meaning or express the same general idea as the sentences below.

1. After goods have been produced, the most efficient method of delivering them to the customer must be determined.
2. The trade channel refers to the route the finished goods travel from the producer to the person who buys them to use.
3. Most of the time the channel of distribution involves middlemen who actually become owners of the merchandise or help to transfer ownership.
4. The middleman buys products for resale from several different manufacturers.
5. An agent middleman receives a fee for bringing buyer and seller together.
6. Convenience goods must be available for sale at many locations.
7. A customer will pay extra if the product is available at a convenient location.
8. In a full service retail store, personal selling can affect sales.
9. The product can generally be seen and demonstrated.
10. In a discount house merchandise can be sold for a lower price because there are not a lot of salesmen, and the costs of operating the store are lower.
11. Discount houses try to move their merchandise fast.
12. A franchise store may be owned by a small business manager who has permission to operate from a larger company.
13. The small business manager pays a certain percentage from his sales to the parent company.
14. If a large company controls the middlemen and the method of transportation, it is vertically integrated.
15. Large business organizations are not always as efficient and profitable as smaller companies.

B: Matching

Match the words below with the definitions. Use Exercise A to help you.

1. bring to market _____ a. company that grants a franchise

2. ultimate consumer _____ b. fee paid for making a sale

3. take possession of _____ c. available for sale at many locations

4. take title to _____ d. deliver to the customer

5. commission _____ e. owning the retail outlet, the distributor and maybe even the producer

6. widely distributed _____ f. able to be seen

7. place utility _____ g. costs other than costs of the product, such as rent, electricity, management

8. personal selling _____ h. legal permission to operate certain businesses

9. on display _____ i. explaining the features of a product to a potential customer

10. overhead _____ j. increased value due to location

11. high volume _____ k. to become the legal owner

12. franchise or license _____ l. person who buys something for his own use

13. parent company _____ m. large company which owns smaller companies

14. franchisor _____ n. large amounts of merchandise being bought and sold quickly

15. vertically integrated _____ o. a large chain of authority and management

16. bureaucracy _____ p. to hold and have physical control over

C: Completion

This exercise is designed to increase vocabulary and reading comprehension. Select the answer that best completes the meaning of the sentence.

1. A grower selling fruit at a roadside stand is an example of
   a. a middleman.   c. producer selling directly to consumer.
   b. a convenience   d. manufacturer selling directly to middle-
   good.   man.

2. A middleman who takes title to the merchandise is an example of
   a. a merchant   c. a distributor.
   middleman.
   b. an agent middle-   d. a customer.
   man.

3. The purchasing agent at an office probably
   a. deals directly with pencil manufacturers.
   b. acts as a middleman.
   c. orders through a local office supply store.
   d. distributes office supplies from his warehouse.

4. A stock broker or real estate broker would be an example of
   a. a person who receives title to certain investments.
   b. a person who deals with both buyer and seller.
   c. a person who buys large quantities of real estate and stock.
   d. a salesman.

5. The best channel of distribution depends on
   a. the type of   c. where the product will be sold.
   product.
   b. the price of the   d. all of these.
   product.

6. The cost of distribution for convenience goods is probably
   a. higher than for   c. not a factor in the sales price.
   shopping goods.
   b. not important   d. part of the commission.
   for the consumer.

7. A full service retail store has higher costs than a discount store because
   a. distribution costs are higher.
   b. shopping goods generally cost more than convenience goods.
   c. the cost of space and the salaries of the sales staff must be taken into account.
   d. the merchandise moves slowly.

8. Discount houses can offer merchandise at lower prices because

   a. they have lower overhead.
   b. they deal in volume.
   c. they have fewer salesmen.
   d. all of the above.

9. Franchise and chain stores benefit from

   a. the sale of licenses to their stores.
   b. locating away from the main business areas.
   c. vertical integration.
   d. the ability to advertise on a large scale.

10. The difference between chain stores and franchise stores is

   a. chain stores are individually owned.
   b. franchise stores are individually owned.
   c. they do not handle similar products.
   d. franchise stores enjoy an advantage in distribution.

Listening and Note-Taking Skills

D: Vocabulary in context

This lesson contains several important terms which have special meanings for business. Many of these terms are defined by the text. Some of them are explained through the use of appositives (nouns, noun phrases, or clauses which follow a noun and are set off by commas); others are illustrated by examples. For example, the second paragraph states, "The channel of distribution or trade channel." The word *or* indicates that the terms *channel of distribution* and *trade channel* are synonymous or have the same meaning. Sometimes the punctuation, the words *or* and *and*, and the phrase *for example* can help us use the context to understand new words and determine their meaning.

   Listen to Paragraphs 2, 3, and 4. The terms listed below are explained in the context. Give the meanings indicated by the context. (The words are in the order in which they appear in the text.)

1. ultimate consumer
2. manufacturer
3. direct sale
4. middlemen
5. take title
6. customer
7. merchant middleman

8. agent middleman

9. convenience goods

10. convenient locations

E: Comprehension questions

Listen to Paragraphs 3 and 4, and answer the following questions.

1. In a direct sale, who sells to the customer?

2. What do we call people who take title to merchandise or arrange for transfer of title?

3. Why do we need middlemen?

4. Who does the middleman buy from?

5. How does he divide the products he purchases?

6. How does he give them place utility?

7. What are two kinds of middlemen?

8. What is another word for an agent middleman?

9. What should be considered when selecting a type of channel of distribution?

10. What does a customer probably consider most important when purchasing an item such as chewing gum?

F: Outlining

Listen to Paragraphs 3–8 and then make an outline of them using the following headings:

   I. Middleman (Paragraph 3)
  II. Convenience Goods (Paragraph 4)
 III. Shopping Goods (Paragraph 5)
 IV. Location of Sale (Paragraph 6)
  V. Discount Houses (Paragraph 7)
 VI. Franchise and chain stores (Paragraph 8)

Reading Comprehension

G: Comprehension questions

This lesson can be divided in two parts. The first part describes the function of distribution from the view of the business manager. The first paragraph states how the need for distribution arises in business. The second paragraph defines the problem in more detail giving examples of the most basic producer-to-consumer transactions and showing the need for a more sophisticated network. Paragraph 3 defines the middleman and his role in distribution. The second part, paragraphs 5, 6, 7, and 8, explains the distribution system from the perspective of the customer. Does the customer want to pay for convenience, or are product characteristics more important? It states how the nature of the product and customer considerations determine the type of distribution. Finally, the large, vertically integrated organizations are mentioned along with their advantages and disadvantages.

In addition to noticing the overall organization of a passage, a careful reader must also pay attention to the details.

Answer the following questions in complete sentences. Use the specific details given in the text.

1. What is a channel of distribution?
2. What is the most general explanation of a middleman?
3. Why is the middleman necessary?
4. What are three specific activities of the middleman?
5. What is a merchant middleman?
6. What is an agent middleman?
7. What does the customer consider when purchasing convenience goods?
8. How are convenience goods distributed?
9. What are convenience goods?
10. What two things do customers consider when they purchase shopping goods?
11. What service does a full service retail store provide the customer?
12. How is a franchise store similar to a chain store?
13. What is a franchise?
14. How is a franchise store different from a chain store?
15. What does it mean if a company is vertically integrated?
16. What advantage do chain stores and franchise stores enjoy?
17. What is meant by a parent company?
18. What services does the parent company supply?
19. What is an advantage of vertical integration?
20. What can be a problem in a vertically integrated enterprise?

Writing

H: Writing a paragraph

Suppose it is your job to arrange for distribution of a product which your company has made. Write a paragraph describing the nature of the product as it relates to the consumer and what should be taken into consideration in distributing it. Here is a list of products which you might want to consider:

1. razor blades
2. refrigerator
3. shoes
4. an article of clothing
5. candy

Vocabulary Review: Rephrasing

I: Rephrasing words and expressions

Rewrite the following sentences. Replace the words and expressions *in italics* with expressions from the text which have the same meaning.

1. The marketer must consider which *channel of distribution* to use for these particular *goods*.
2. Sometimes a product may go through several *distributors* before it reaches the *person who buys and uses it himself*.
3. The *person who buys supplies for the office* likes to find a store *close to where he works*.
4. A merchant middleman may *deliver* goods from his *storage building* to *many stores where customers shop*.
5. An *agent middleman* receives a *fee* for bringing buyer and seller together.
6. Agent middlemen arrange for *changes of ownership*.
7. At the retail store the product *can be seen*.
8. The sales staff explains *the characteristics* of the product and *shows how it works*.
9. Discount houses usually have lower *costs of operation*.
10. Customers usually shop around before purchasing large expensive *household electrical devices* like refrigerators and television sets.

11. Chain stores sometimes *control many aspects of production and distribution.*

12. Large business organizations are sometimes characterized by the *inability to adapt.*

13. A large company is able to *make the most profits.*

14. Before you can operate a MacDonald's, you must get *permission* from the main company.

15. Discount houses carry only merchandise *which they can sell quickly.*

Oral Practice

Debate

Resolved: To eliminate all unnecessary sales staff in retail stores. A retail outlet that can cut its costs has an unquestionable advantage over its competition. Therefore, a large sales staff is an unnecessary expense, and should be reduced to a minimum. (Discuss the arguments for and against this. Be sure you consider all types of retail outlets.)

Glossary for Lesson Seven
Distribution

Agent: a person who represents another person or company for the purpose of conducting business.

The Mutual Insurance Company has ten thousand *agents* nationwide who sell insurance and settle claims.

Broker: an agent middleman who arranges for contracts of purchase and sale.

My stock *broker* advised me to purchase some stock in that new company.

If you wish to purchase that building, you should contact a real estate *broker.*

Bureaucracy: a large, sometimes inefficient corporate or government structure.

This corporation has gotten so big that it is very difficult to find out who is really responsible for certain aspects of the company. The large *bureaucracy* prevents management from taking quick action to solve problems.

Chain: a group of associated stores or businesses having the same name and sharing certain features.

Most *chain* stores are owned by a large corporation known as the parent company. K-Mart and Sears are two of the world's largest retail *chains*.

Channel of distribution: the route or way that a product travels from the manufacturer to the consumer. It includes all the middlemen, transportation companies, warehouses, and others.

The *channel of distribution* for convenience goods such as cigarettes can involve several middlemen.

Commission: the money or fee which a salesman receives for making a sale.

A salesman usually receives a *commission* for each sale. The more he sells, the more money he receives.

Some salesmen receive *commissions* as high as 20% of the sales price.

Convenience goods: products that are usually inexpensive and purchased at the most convenient location.

In a large store, *convenience goods* are often found close to the checkout stand.

Examples of *convenience goods* are cigarettes, chewing gum, and soft drinks.

Distribution: refers to the business activity that delivers products to locations convenient for the customer.

Distribution is an important consideration for the Coca-Cola Company. If a potential customer cannot easily find a Coke, he may purchase a Pepsi instead.

Features: characteristics of a product.

The salesman was demonstrating the *features* of the microwave oven.

Flexibility: ability to adapt and change.

General purpose machines have greater *flexibility* than specialized machines.

Smaller companies sometimes have greater *flexibility* than large corporations because changes involve fewer people.

Franchise: legal permission from a large company to use their name or logo and to sell their products.

You need to purchase a *franchise* from MacDonald's if you want to open a MacDonald's restaurant.

Franchisee: one who buys a franchise.

Franchisor: one who grants a franchise.

Home appliance: an electrical device used for performing household work.

Small *appliances* such as electric irons and toasters do not use as much electricity as major *appliances* such as washing machines and dryers.

Inflexibility: inability to change, opposite of flexibility.

The *inflexibility* resulting from a large corporate structure prevents the company from responding quickly to changes in market forces.

License: legal permission to perform certain business activities.

A franchise is similar to a *license*.

This bottler has obtained a *license* from Coca-Cola Inc., to bottle and distribute Coke.

Maximize: increase, make as large as possible.

If one company controls all aspects of production, distribution, and sales, it has an opportunity to *maximize* profits.

Merchandise: goods for sale at a store or in transport to a place of sale.

The fire at the store caused considerable damage to the building and the *merchandise*.

Middleman: a person or a company which takes possession of merchandise or arranges for transfer of ownership or merchandise in the channel of distribution.

A merchant *middleman* actually buys products and controls their ownership.

An agent *middleman* arranges for buyers and sellers to get together and conduct business.

Outlet: actual location where the ultimate consumer makes his purchase.

Retail *outlets* include supermarkets, department stores, and discount stores.

Overhead: costs of doing business other than the direct costs of the raw materials or merchandise.

In a supermarket *overhead* costs include the cost of the building, the salaries of the employees, the cost of advertising, and the cost of utilities such as electricity used to run the lights and refrigerators.

Ownership: legal rights a person has to property that belongs to him.

Transfer of *ownership* means change of ownership.

The middleman arranges for the transfer of *ownership*.

Parent company: a large corporation which may own several smaller companies or stores.

General Motors Corporation is the *parent company* of Fisher Body Works.

Possession: actual physical control over property; to take possession means to occupy.

After you have signed all the papers and given us the money for the purchase, you can then take *possession* of the building.

Produce (noun) (pronounced pró duce): fresh fruits and vegetables.

I bought these apples at a *produce* stand by the side of the road.

Promote: to encourage the development of some business activity—usually sales.

The parent company will help the franchise stores *promote* their sales.

Retail: purchase of products for personal use as opposed to purchasing them for resale.

Retail stores usually purchase a lot of advertising space in newspapers.

Route: a path or selected course of travel, a channel.

Fresh fruits and vegetables should travel the most direct *route* to the consumer so that there is the least chance of spoilage.

Shopping goods: products which customers purchase only after consideration of many factors and usually after comparing the quality and price with similar products.

Home appliances are considered *shopping goods* since a customer will usually go out of his way to buy what he considers the best product for the price.

Stand: a small, open-air shop for the purchase of convenience goods.

I bought this newspaper at the newspaper *stand*. You can get a sandwich and a coke at the lunch *stand*.

Title: a legal document that shows legal ownership.

The merchant middleman actually takes *title* to the merchandise.

Transfer: to change ownership of property from one person to another.

The agent middleman arranges for *transfer* of ownership from seller to buyer.

Ultimate consumer: a person who buys a product for his own personal use, not for resale or use in business.

When I purchase food at the supermarket, I am the *ultimate consumer* of the product.

The man who bottles the wine in France has no idea who the *ultimate consumer* will be.

Vending machine: a coin-operated machine that sells convenience goods.

I got this candy from the *vending machine*.

Vertical integration: business structure in which a parent company owns the means of production, distribution, and final sale.

Vertical integration in the oil industry means that the same large companies own the wells, the refineries, the delivery trucks, and the service stations.

Because of *vertical integration*, oil companies can control the price of gasoline at the pumps.

Volume: quantity.

A high *volume* retailer is one who buys and sells a great quantity of products.

This retailer can offer you a lower price because he deals in *volume*.

Warehouse: a building where merchandise is stored on the distribution channel.

The salesman said that he did not have any more washing machines in stock, but that there were some at the company *warehouse*.

Wholesaler: a merchant middleman who sells goods to retailers in large quantities.

Wholesalers in the oil industry purchase gasoline from refineries for delivery to service stations.

Clothing *wholesalers* sell hundreds of shirts and blouses to retail department stores.

Introduction to Lesson Eight: Promotion

The lesson on promotion begins with a discussion of the theoretical basis for promotion. It is related to the basic economic law of supply and demand. Practical application of the law is then discussed. Many fields can be used in promotional activity, for example, statistics and psychology, and reference is made to these areas in this introduction. The vocabulary is rich in words and phrases about human behavior related to directing consumer choices.

Besides marketing and promotional theories, the nature of the product and its intended market are discussed. The student should acquire the ability to generalize and ask broad questions in order to determine the problems connected with promoting a specific product and to conceive of solutions for those problems. For example, the marketer should ask, "Who are the potential customers for a particular product?" "How do we communicate with those potential customers?" Formulating questions about basic general goals and problems involves the ability to differentiate between details and generalizations, which is an excellent problem-solving tool for the business manager in every field of business. The reading comprehension exercises emphasize practical applications of theoretical concepts.

The listening and note-taking exercises require the student to determine which of the various media discussed are most suitable for advertising particular products. There is thus further emphasis on application of the material.

Linguistic concepts useful for this lesson include suffixes, abstract nouns, metaphors, introductory phrases, and conjunctions.

One purpose of promotion is to keep customers and potential customers aware of the company name and the service it provides. Sante Fe marks its trucks, trains, and containers with its logo (a cross inside a circle) and the services it provides.

8

Promotion

The Role and Activities of Promotion

Paragraph 1

Promotion is the aspect of marketing concerned with increasing sales. Marketing must be considered in making production decisions, and promotion must be considered in the overall marketing process. Promotion attempts to persuade and influence the customer's attitude in various ways. It is oriented toward producing a customer for the product rather than a product for the customer. Economists believe price should be determined by supply and demand. Promotion attempts to increase demand for a product and thereby increase sales. It wants to make the

unchangeable demand for a product <u>inelastic</u> when prices increase and elastic when prices decrease. In other words, through promotion, companies try to keep demand and sales constant when prices increase. They do not want an increase in the price of their product to result in lower sales; instead they want it to result in an increase in profits. However, if the price decreases, they want demand for the product to increase, hoping that an

balance increase in sales volume will <u>offset</u> the decrease in price.

Meet your Orange County market in The Times.

The Times Orange County Edition is a great way for you to reach the top consumers in your growing marketing area. Every weekday, for example, we deliver a large Orange County audience of 421,200. On Sunday, we reach 488,000 adult readers. And every day of the week your messages will go to 54% of all Orange County adults with household incomes of $35,000 and over ... more than any other paper in Orange County.

Because the tastes and interests of our readers are as diverse as the Orange County market itself, we publish special local advertising and editorial throughout the week —throughout The Times. Specifically for Orange County. Each opens up an important segment of your market. Effectively and consistently.

Part II	Local advertising and editorial	Monday-Saturday
Sports	Local advertising and editorial	Monday-Saturday
View	Local advertising and editorial	Monday-Saturday
Business	Local advertising and editorial	Tuesday, Wednesday and Friday
Classified	Local advertising	Daily
Food	Local advertising	Thursday
Fashion 82	Local advertising	Friday
Calendar	Local advertising and editorial	Friday
Orange County	Local advertising and editorial	Sunday

For details on maximizing your advertising effectiveness in Orange County, call The Times at 957-2000.

The Times Orange County Edition

Newspaper advertising can be targeted for specific geographical areas.

Paragraph 2

Three main promotional activities are advertising, personal selling, and sales promotion. Advertising is a nonpersonal presentation of goods, services, or ideas aimed at a mass audience. It is particularly suited for products that are widely distributed, such as convenience goods. There are several methods of advertising and several <u>media</u>. The method selected depends upon the product, <u>the distribution of the market</u>, and the type of information which the company wishes to <u>convey</u> about its product. For example, television advertising reaches a large audience. It has the advantage of appealing to the emotions of the audience through the senses of sight and sound. Television advertisements are expensive to produce and must be repeated thousands of times in order to justify the cost of production. Newspaper advertisements, on the other hand, can appear on a particular day in a particular geographic area. A newspaper advertisement can contain a lot of written detail that appeals to the logic of the reader. It explains why he should purchase a particular product or service.

Paragraph 3

In general, advertising works best when the demand for a product is increasing. It also works well when there are real differences between two or more similar products such as the different types of cars. Using advertising, a company can emphasize the differences between its product and that of the competition. The purpose of advertising is to communicate information that convinces a customer to buy a specific product.

Paragraph 4

Personal selling involves a salesperson trying to convince customers directly to buy a product. Personal selling is very effective when there is a concentrated market for a product—in other words, the product is not for general consumption by the public. For example, airplanes are purchased only by airlines, not by the general public. There would be little point in advertising them on television. The same is true for many industrial goods. A sales representative usually gets a commission. If the product has a high unit value, in other words each individual item is very expensive, the cost of the product justifies the commission paid to the sales representative for his or her work. If the product must be individually <u>tailored to</u> the purchaser, the salesperson must be able to sell exactly what the customer needs. Sales staff are also needed to demonstrate a product. This is particularly important for new products which may be unfamiliar to the customer. Finally, personal selling is necessary when there is negotiation about the price of the product, for example, when a trade-in is involved.

means of communication; the type of people who will buy the product; communicate

designed for

Paragraph 5

Sales promotion involves several activities. It is becoming increasingly important in the self-service environment where there is often no sales staff. Sales promotion activities are of two types: information and stimulation. Examples of information promotion are a pamphlet or booklet about the product, a demonstration, market research information telling about the nature of the customers, and dealer training and managerial advice from producers. Stimulation promotion can be accomplished by the distribution of free samples, reduced price promotions, premiums, and coupons. A premium is something that the customer receives as a bonus when he purchases a product. For example, a customer purchasing a razor might receive a free package of razor blades. A coupon is a certificate which entitles the customer to purchase the product at a reduced price. Sales promotions also involve displays of the products. Displays can increase sales as well. A customer might make a decision to buy a particular product like a convenience item simply on the basis of a display that makes the item easy to see and reach.

Paragraph 6

looking for

Basically there are two ways to increase sales of products: find new markets and increase market share. A company <u>seeking</u> new markets can expand its geographical sales area or try to sell its product to a different segment of the population. In this case promotion may involve increased advertising to spread information about the product. Personal selling at the wholesale level can encourage additional retailers to <u>carry</u> the product.

have in their stores for sale

Paragraph 7

attract

A different market situation requires a different method of promotion. When a market is saturated, it means that there are no new customers to be found. A company then needs to <u>lure</u> customers from the competition and gain a greater share of the total market. To increase market share, the marketing department of a company must design a total program of promotion for a particular product. Such a program may involve increased advertising to remind the customer of the name of the product. In advertising the company will also emphasize the superiority of its product by comparing it with the competition's product. A program to increase market share may also include convincing a retailer to allow

display area

more <u>shelf space</u> in the store for the product. Sales promotions may include contests, coupons, and price discounting. Increasing market share involves more stimulation of the buyer's emotions than does finding new markets where simply furnishing information about the product may increase sales.

Vocabulary Building Introduction

A: Vocabulary in context

Study the following sentences. Pay attention to the words in *italics*.

1. Promotion attempts to increase demand for a product, which is represented graphically as a *shift* in the demand curve. The *demand curve* expresses the relationship between price and the quantity demanded. When the price decreases, more people will purchase the product.

2. When the price *decreases*, more people will purchase the product. The *demand* for the product is *elastic*. More people desire to own the product when the price is lower.

3. We want people to continue to *desire* and purchase the product even when the price increases. When the price increases, we do not want *demand* to change. Demand should be *inelastic* when the price increases. We want demand and sales to be *constant* even when the price increases. We don't want sales to *fall off*.

4. If the sales increase when the price is lowered, the increase in sales will *offset* the decrease in price. High *sales volume* will make up for the decrease in profit per item. There is a lower profit made on each item, but the increase in the number of items sold *compensates* for the lower profit per item. *Overall* profits have remained *constant*. The total profit is the same.

5. Promotion attempts to *persuade* and *influence* the customer's attitude. Promotion tries to make the customer *think differently* about the product. As a result of effective promotion the customer forms a good *opinion* about the product. The customer has favorable thoughts about the product.

6. Advertising is a *nonpersonal* presentation of goods, services, or ideas aimed at a *mass audience*. Advertising is nonpersonal because every person sees the exact same advertisement. The advertisement is not *tailored* for the individual. The advertiser wants a *maximum number* of people to see or read his message. He *aims at* a mass audience.

7. Advertising is *suited* to products which are *widely* distributed. Advertising is a good way to sell *convenience* goods. Television and newspapers are two advertising *media*. Radio is another *medium*.

8. We should choose a method based on the *distribution of the market*. Most people who buy winter clothes live in cold climates. The market is distributed *geographically*. You can sell winter clothes in *areas* where there are cold winters.

9. Most movie goers are between the ages of 16 and 25. The market for movies is distributed *demographically*. People who spend money for movies are mostly a *certain age*. The advertiser must know how the market is *distributed*.

10. Television advertising *appeals* to the senses of *sight* and *sound*. *Audiences* see and hear television advertisements. Newspaper advertisements appear on certain days in certain areas. They have *time utility* and geographical distribution.

B: Matching

Try to match the words on the left with words and phrases having the same meaning.

1. shift	_____ a . consumer desire to purchase product
2. demand curve	_____ b . arrangement
3. supply	_____ c . according to population
4. decreases	_____ d . according to location
5. demand	_____ e . price-demand relationship expressed as a graph
6. elastic	_____ f . usefulness at a certain time
7. constant	_____ g . maximum number of viewers or readers
8. fall off	_____ h . be appropriate
9. inelastic	_____ i . compensate for
10. offset	_____ j . quantity of items available for sale
11. sales volume	_____ k . opinion
12. overall	_____ l . able to change under certain conditions
13. persuade	_____ m. becomes less

14. attitude ＿＿＿ n . methods to convey information

15. nonpersonal ＿＿＿ o . decline

16. mass audience ＿＿＿ p . total

17. suited ＿＿＿ q . change

18. media ＿＿＿ r . convince

19. distribution ＿＿＿ s . rate of sales

20. demographic ＿＿＿ t . unresponsive to increasing prices

21. geographic ＿＿＿ u . unchangeable

22. time utility ＿＿＿ v . mass

Vocabulary Building and Reading Comprehension

C: Multiple choice

This exercise is designed to increase vocabulary and reading comprehension. Select the answer which best completes the meaning of the sentence.

1. Promotion attempts to increase demand for the product. Effective promotion therefore
   a. increases sales. c. aims at a mass audience.
   b. decreases supply. d. decreases prices.

2. Promotion should shift the demand curve so that
   a. supplies increase. c. consumers want to buy the product more than before.
   b. prices increase. d. demand stays constant.

3. If the demand for the product is inelastic, when prices increase
   a. customers continue to buy the product even at higher prices.
   b. increased prices result in fewer sales.
   c. increased prices result in more sales.
   d. the supply available for sale is increased.

4. If customers increase purchases of the product when prices decrease,
   a. sales volume increases.
   b. the demand is elastic.
   c. increased volume may offset lower prices.
   d. all of the above.

5. Advertising is aimed at a mass audience. Advertisers hope
   a. that it will be convenient for the customer to purchase the product.
   b. that a very great number of people will see or hear their message.
   c. that reducing prices will increase sales.
   d. to sell similar products.

6. Television and radio are examples of advertising media. A newspaper
   a. must be widely distributed in order to be useful for advertisers.
   b. is a different type of medium.
   c. cannot tell you what day the advertisement will appear.
   d. usually cannot convey detailed information about the product.

7. Television advertisements are usually very expensive to produce. Because of their cost
   a. they should not be used to promote convenience goods.
   b. they usually appear only on a certain day in a certain area.
   c. they are especially good for expensive products like airplanes.
   d. they must be shown thousands of times.

8. Personal selling refers to a sales representative who persuades a customer to buy a product. It is very effective when
   a. the product must be custom designed for the customer.
   b. the number of customers is small and the sales staff know who they are.
   c. the product needs to be demonstrated to the customer.
   d. all of the above.

9. A commission refers to a fee which the salesperson receives for making a sale. A commission is usually based on a certain percentage of the sales price. Sales staff probably
   a. prefer to sell expensive or big ticket items since their commission will be greater.
   b. prefer to sell convenience items since customers purchase them frequently.
   c. can afford to advertise on television to demonstrate their product.
   d. are unable to negotiate the price of the product.

10. In a self-service store the customer usually selects merchandise personally and then brings it to a cashier to pay for it. Self-service stores

a. could probably increase sales if they used personal selling.
b. can stimulate sales by the proper use of displays and other sales promotion devices.
c. cannot use advertising effectively.
d. usually sell only convenience items.

11. Sales promotion activities include those which provide information to customers and those which stimulate them to purchase particular products. Customers receive information about products through

a. coupons.   c. premiums.
b. pamphlets.   d. discounts.

12. A customer can be stimulated to make a purchase through

a. a free sample.   c. a reduced price.
b. an attractive   d. all of the above.
   and convenient
   display.

13. Increasing sales means getting more customers for your product. You can get more customers to buy your product by finding new markets. A method of expanding the market might be

a. to sell your product in other cities and states.
b. to sell your product to people who do not now purchase your product or a similar product.
c. advertising to tell more people about your product.
d. all of the above.

14. You can also get more customers for your product if they switch from a competing brand to your own. To do this requires

a. only getting more products on the shelves at the store.
b. giving more information about your product.
c. saturating the market.
d. designing a total program according to the product and the market.

15. The promotional activities of a company can best be carried out

a. if a complete advertising program is designed.
b. if dealers are properly trained.
c. if demand for the product is increasing.
d. if it is considered as part of the total marketing process.

Listening and Note-Taking Skills

D: Vocabulary in context

While many of the words here may already be familiar in another context, they have a particular meaning in business. For example, the word *elastic* used in the first paragraph may be familiar in its concrete sense meaning *rubber-like*. However, in this chapter it and many other words are used in an abstract or more general sense. The abstract meanings can be learned by understanding the main idea of the paragraph and using the context. Examples and explanations are given. Look for phrases such as *for example* and *in other words*. Phrases that indicate a comparison or opposite meaning may help in the understanding of a concept. Phrases such as *on the other hand* and words like *however* and *but* indicate such contrasts.

Listen to the first two paragraphs and try to understand the meaning of the following terms. In your own words or using the words given in the text, try to write an explanation of each term.

1. shift the demand curve
2. keep sales constant
3. elastic demand
4. sales volume
5. offset
6. promotion
7. presentation
8. aimed at
9. media
10. wide audience
11. justify
12. demand

E: Comprehension questions

Listen to Paragraphs 2, 3, and 4 and answer the following questions.

1. Which promotional activity is best suited for convenience goods?
2. Who should receive the advertiser's message?
3. When selecting a medium, what are two things which should be considered?
4. Which medium appeals through sight and sound?

5. Why are television advertisements repeated so often?
6. What medium can provide detail?
7. Who does personal selling?
8. Provide an example of a product sold through personal selling.
9. What is paid to the sales staff?
10. Suggest two services besides personal selling that the sales staff can perform.

F: Outlining

Listen again to Paragraphs 2, 3, 4, and 5 and make an outline of them.

Reading Comprehension

G: Comprehension questions

In trying to remember what we read it is useful to notice the general organization of the material. This particular lesson is organized in seven parts, which correspond to the seven paragraphs:

1. promotion and its goals
2. types of promotional activities
3. the best situations for advertising and the purpose of advertising
4. personal selling
5. sales promotion activities
6. ways of increasing sales
7. ways to increase market share

Keeping in mind the overall organization of the lesson, read Paragraphs 4, 5, 6, and 7 and answer the following questions.

1. Why is personal selling effective in a concentrated market?
2. Why is advertising probably not effective for the sale of industrial goods?
3. Why would personal selling be effective for expensive shopping goods?
4. Why is a salesperson necessary when there is a trade in?
5. What is one difference between sales promotion and personal selling?
6. Which sales promotional activity is similar to personal selling? How is it similar?

7. How would you classify free samples, premiums, and coupons as types of sales promotions?

8. What's the difference between a premium and a coupon?

9. How can displays increase the sales of convenience items?

10. What are two sources of new customers for a product?

11. How might increased advertising help to expand the market?

12. How might advertising help increase market share?

13. What are two personal selling activities of the wholesaler?

14. What kinds of sales promotional activities are aimed at increasing market share?

15. How should a company decide which promotional activities to use?

Writing

H: Writing a planned paragraph

Suppose you were in charge of the marketing division of a company that produced soft drinks or another convenience product. You now market your product in a large metropolitan area, but want to increase the sales of this product. What are some promotional activities you could consider and why?

Write a paragraph or paragraphs according to this plan. First, explain your current market situation. Then explain how you intend to attract more customers. Finally, explain how such activities will accomplish your goal.

Vocabulary Review: Rephrasing

I: Rephrasing expressions

Rewrite the following sentences. Replace the words and expressions in *italics* with expressions from the text which have the same meaning.

1. From economic theory we know that price should be determined by the *quantity available for sale* and the *desire for the product* on the part of customers.

2. Promotion attempts to shift the *relationship between supply and demand* to increase demand and sales.

3. Ideally, demand and sales should *stay constant* when prices increase.

4. They hope that an *increase in the number of units sold* will *compensate for* a decrease in prices.

5. Promotion attempts to *urge* the customer to buy the product.

6. Advertising is *useful* for products which are *available in many places.*

7. The company wants to *present* certain information *about* its product.

8. *Commercial messages on television* are seen by *many viewers.*

9. Television and radio are two *channels of communication* for advertising.

10. Newspaper advertisements *have time value*, and they can be *delivered in specific communities.*

11. Using advertising, a company can *point out* the differences between their product and that of *another company which produces a similar product.*

12. Personal selling is effective when *there are just certain purchasers for the product.*

13. Airplanes are not purchased by *most consumers.*

14. The cost is high enough so that the producer *can afford to pay* the salesperson a *fee.*

15. Sometimes the product must be *specifically designed* for the purchaser.

16. The salesperson is necessary when there is *discussion* about the price.

17. The purchase of a new car sometimes involves *the exchange* of an older model.

18. The salesperson can *show* the customer *how* the product *works.*

19. Here is some information *about the type of customers who purchase this product.*

20. If you purchase this brand of toothpaste, you will receive a toothbrush as a *free gift.*

21. The customer decided to purchase this product because *it was easy to see and reach.*

22. This *certificate*, which you can cut out of the magazine, allows you to purchase the product at a reduced price.

23. We want to encourage the *store owners* to *have* our product *available for sale.*

24. If we want *our competitor's customers to purchase our product,* we have to get the retailer to grant us more *area for display.*

25. We have to *influence* the customer to purchase our product.

Oral Practice

Debate

Resolved: Saturating the market with advertising for a product is the best way to increase sales. (Discuss the arguments for and against this.)

Glossary for Lesson Eight
Promotion

Aimed at: intended for, directed at.

Advertising is *aimed at* many listeners and readers.

Certificate: a piece of paper or document having a certain value.

This gift *certificate* is worth $10.00. It can be exchanged for merchandise worth $10.00.

Commission: a fee or payment which a salesman receives for making a sale.

Commissions are usually based on a certain percentage of the selling price. This salesman receives a 20% *commission*. If he sells something for $1000, his *commission* is $200.

Competition: when two or more companies try to get a customer; also, another company which makes a similar product.

General Motors and Ford are in *competition* to sell cars.

A good marketing division knows what the *competition* is doing.

In making plans for sales promotion, a company must consider the *competition*.

Concentrated market also **market concentration:** situation in which there are very few customers for the product.

There is a *concentrated market* for high voltage transformers. Usually only electric utility companies purchase them.

Constant: unchanging or unchanged.

Promotion attempts to keep sales *constant* even when prices increase. The company wants to sell the same number of items at higher prices.

Convey: to transfer from one place or from one person to another.

Advertising *conveys* information about the product.

Coupon: a certificate which is usually cut out of a newspaper or magazine advertisement and which allows a customer to purchase a product at a lower price.

Demand curve: a line graph which shows the relationship between price and the quantity demanded.

Promotion attempts to increase sales independently of supply and price, which will be shown on a graph as a shift in the *demand curve*.

Demonstrate: to show how a product, usually a machine, works.

The salesperson will *demonstrate* some of the features of the new computer.

Discount: a reduction in the price, usually for the purpose of increasing sales.

If you purchase 100 units of this product, you will receive a 10% *discount* off the total cost.

Display: an arrangement of merchandise for the purpose of showing it to customers and stimulating sales.

The shoe store has the different styles of shoes on *display*.

If a product is not on *display*, a customer may not know that it is available.

A store manager usually *displays* convenience items.

Effective: having desirable results.

Advertising in newspapers is not an *effective* way of selling aircraft. Personal selling is more *effective* for aircraft sales.

We have had an *effective* sales promotion campaign. Sales have increased 10% over last year.

Elastic: able to change and respond to certain forces.

Demand should be *elastic* when prices decline. A decline in prices should increase sales.

Free sample: a small amount of a product distributed to potential customers at no charge.

Distributing *free samples* is sometimes an effective way to stimulate sales of new products.

General public: includes most people in a society, a mass market.

Food products are sold to the *general public*, while raw materials are usually sold only to businesses who can produce something with them.

These records and tapes are not available to the *general public*; you can receive them only when you join our record and tape club.

Geographic: refers to the location of communities and customers.

Since newspapers are usually local enterprises, newspaper advertising can be aimed at certain *geographic* areas.

These winter clothes are marketed *geographically*. We sell them in areas where the winter weather is cold.

Industrial goods: products which are produced and sold to companies who use them in their businesses.

Computers used to be considered only as *industrial* goods, but now companies are marketing small home computers to the general public.

Inelastic: unchangeable, unresponsive to changes in conditions.

When prices increase, we want sales to remain constant; we want demand to be *inelastic*.

Influence: to change a person's mind, to have an effect on.

Advertising attempts to *influence* the customers' buying habits so that they will purchase the product being advertised.

Justify: to prove or show that something is reasonable.

The company can *justify* the cost of the salesperson's commission because the unit price of the item is very high. We can *justify* paying a person $100 to sell a product worth $1000.

These promotional activities have not increased sales. They have only reduced profits. We cannot *justify* continuing them.

Lure: attract.

The high price of motor fuel has *lured* customers away from big automobiles which use a lot of gasoline.

If we want to increase market share, we have to *lure* customers away from our competitor's product.

Market research: information about the characteristics of the customers who purchase the products.

Market research indicates that customers who purchase large automobiles have large families and usually earn higher than average salaries.

Market share: among competitors, one company's percentage of the total sales for a certain type of product.

This month 100,000 automobiles were sold in the United States. 32,000 of those automobiles were produced by General Motors. General Motors has a 32% *market share*.

With its new marketing program, Coca-Cola hopes to increase its share of the soft drink market. Miller Brewing Company increased its *market share* with an advertising campaign.

Medium (pl, **media**): a method of communicating information.

Newspapers and television are news and advertising *media*.

As an advertising *medium*, radio is less expensive than television.

Negotiation: business discussion for the purpose of reaching an agreement.

After an hour of *negotiation*, we agreed on a price.

A salesperson is able to do some *negotiation* about the price.

Offset: to balance or to make up for, to compensate for.

The decrease in the number of units sold has been *offset* by an increase in the price of each unit. Therefore, the sales figure has not changed.

Pamphlet: brochure, a folded paper or small book which gives information about a product.

This *pamphlet* will describe the features and characteristics of this stereo system.

Persuade: influence, convince.

A good display location can *persuade* a customer to purchase a certain convenience product.

The salesperson *persuaded* me that the more expensive product was superior.

The young woman was *persuaded* by the salesman to buy a used car.

Premium: a bonus or additional item which a customer receives at no extra cost when he purchases a certain item.

If you purchase this camera, you will receive two rolls of film at no additional cost. You receive two rolls of film as a *premium* when you purchase the camera.

Promotion: marketing activity intended to increase demand and sales of products.

Because of good *promotion* programs, we have increased sales 10% this year.

Sales: transactions involving receiving money for products.

We have increased the number of *sales* through advertising.

Sales volume: the quantity of sales.

Sales volume has increased since the prices were reduced.

Saturated: a market situation in which all the customers have made their purchases and there are no new customers to be found.

The market for wrist watches is almost completely *saturated*, but we expect to increase our sales of pocket calculators.

Segment: part.

If we cannot increase sales by luring customers from our competition, then we should try to sell to a different *segment* of the population.

Our advertising has been aimed at that *segment* of the population between the ages of 20 and 35. Let's try to get older people to purchase our product too.

Self service: type of retail store where the customers select their merchandise without the help of sales staff and bring it to the cashier.

Supermarkets are examples of *self-service* stores.

Displays are a method of stimulating sales in *self-service* stores.

Shelf space: area available for display of products in retail stores.

If General Mills can convince the retailers to grant them more *shelf space*, they can increase sales of their breakfast cereals.

Stimulation: convincing or encouraging a customer to buy a product.

If advertising can keep the name of the product in the customer's mind, he will be *stimulated* to purchase that product when he sees it.

Tailored: custom designed for a particular customer.

The type of insurance you purchase should be *tailored* to your own particular situation.

Personal selling is effective when the product is *tailored* to the particular customer.

Trade-in: an older or used product which is being exchanged for a newer model.

This 1965 Volkswagen was used as a *trade-in* on a new Toyota.

The salesperson will allow me $100 for my *trade-in*.

Unfamiliar: unknown.

The salesperson will show you how to use this new microwave oven if you are *unfamiliar* with it.

Unit value: the cost, price, or value of one individual item.

Automobiles have a high *unit value*. Soft drinks have a low *unit value*. One car costs a lot of money. One soft drink is relatively inexpensive.

Wide audience: mass market, a large population exposed to media advertising.

Television advertising is aimed at a *wide audience*. Many people will see the commercial message on television.

Introduction to Lesson Nine:
Financial Statements

Lesson Nine discusses the most important financial statement of a business, the balance sheet. The balance sheet has been selected because it is a standard financial document for almost all businesses since it deals with the area of accounting.

The lesson begins with a definition of financial statements and then proceeds to analyze the balance sheet. A good way for the student to remember the material discussed in this chapter would be either to visualize the right and left sides of the balance sheet or to draw a diagram of a balance sheet according to the description given. The two sides of the balance sheet should help the student distinguish and remember the meanings of words because the juxtaposed terms are opposites, e.g., current assets vs. current liabilities; owes vs. owns.

Three ways of thinking are emphasized in this lesson. One is analysis, or the examination of the parts of the balance sheet. A second is classification: the student sees that items are grouped together on the balance sheet according to shared characteristics. Finally, there is comparison and contrast between the two basic groupings of items because they share certain common characteristics, yet they are opposite, being either assets or liabilities.

Linguistic concepts useful for Lesson Nine are conjunctions and compound sentences, prepositions of location or position, antonyms, and suffixes.

Financial Statements

The Types and Purposes of Financial Records

Paragraph 1

All businesses need to maintain financial records in order to find out if they are making a profit. These records exist in several forms. In daily business operations recordings of business transactions are first made in a journal. This journal is sometimes called the book of original entry. In the journal, bookkeepers record sales, uses of raw materials, and purchases. Periodically, bookkeepers transfer figures from the journals to ledgers. This activity is known as posting. The ledger is a book containing all the accounts of a company. An account is a financial record which contains information about a group of similar transactions. For example, all sales activities are recorded in one account. Another account may be a record of all the costs of raw materials.

Paragraph 2

Once, bookkeeping served as a good method of determining whether or not a company was making profits and whether or not it owed any

Boston University
student and profes-
sor examine a
computer printout.

records taxes. Small business owners could keep their own <u>books</u> and make business decisions based on the information found there. Nowadays, a more sophisticated system of accounting is needed. The design, maintenance, and interpretation of the information recorded in accounts is referred to as accounting. Accountants use the information in accounts to construct financial statements. These statements are analyzed by management and used as a basis for business decisions such as allocation of financial resources, development of new products, and expansion of operations. The most important of these financial statements are the balance sheet and the statement of income and expenses. These statements are also used for determining income tax liabilities. Income-expense statements for different types of businesses vary greatly. This lesson will discuss only the balance sheet, which is more standard in form.

Paragraph 3

The balance sheet is a financial statement which indicates the condition of a company on a specific date. It is called a balance sheet because it expresses the basic accounting formula: Assets = Liabilities + Owners' Equity. (Owners' equity is sometimes referred to as net worth.) The left side of the balance sheet itemizes the firm's assets. Assets are anything of value to a company. On a balance sheet the value is always expressed in terms of money. Companies have different types of assets. They are usually divided into two groups: current assets and fixed assets.

Paragraph 4

money that is Current assets are either cash or items which will be turned into cash
owed a company during the current business period, such as merchandise to be sold and
easily payments to be received. In addition to cash, inventories, and <u>receivables</u>, companies sometimes have stocks and bonds. These are referred to as securities. All of these assets, such as cash and those <u>readily</u> turned into cash, are known as liquid assets. If a company needs to have more cash
sell for one reason or another, it can <u>liquidate</u> some of its stocks and bonds. On the other hand, merchandise which is not selling quickly because there is not much demand is not very liquid, even though it is considered as current assets.

Paragraph 5

Fixed assets are those that will be kept and used for a long time. Fixed
listed assets are usually <u>itemized</u> according to their use to the firm. New machinery and production equipment are valued at their cost. As the equipment is used, its value decreases. This decrease in value is called
kept on depreciation. Used equipment is therefore <u>carried on</u> the books at origi-

nal cost less depreciation. Depreciation is usually calculated on a yearly basis by dividing the total cost of the equipment by the number of years of useful life. For example, a taxicab may cost $12,000 when new. The taxicab owner may use it for three years and then he will have to purchase a new one. The depreciation on the taxicab is $4,000 per year. Therefore, after one year the value of the taxicab on the balance sheet would be $12,000 – $4,000 = $8,000. After two years it would be $12,000 – $8,000 = $4,000. There are various formulae and methods used for calculating depreciation. The depreciation schedule may be part of the income tax laws of a country.

Paragraph 6

Other fixed assets are furniture and fixtures. Fixtures refer to equipment that is attached to the building. There are light fixtures and plumbing fixtures. Fixtures would also include items such as shelves and air-conditioning and heating equipment. Buildings are another fixed asset. On the balance sheet the value of fixtures and buildings would also indicate accumulated depreciation. Land is also a fixed asset, but its value does not decline, and so it shows no depreciation.

Paragraph 7

The opposite side of the balance sheet shows the liabilities. These are amounts which the company owes. Companies owe money to banks who supply credit to employees whom they haven't yet paid, to governments for taxes, and to other companies who have sold them goods which they haven't yet paid for. Liabilities, like assets, are divided into two groups. Current liabilities are debts which must be paid during the current business cycle. They would include accounts payable, taxes payable, <u>accrued</u> wages payable, and interest on borrowed money. Companies also have long term liabilities. These are debts which do not have to be repaid for perhaps ten, twenty, or thirty years. Companies usually have to pay interest on long term debts. The debts may be in the form of bonds, which are securities sold to banks or other investors, or a mortgage, which is money borrowed from banks for the purpose of purchasing property or equipment. The payment of bonds is usually guaranteed by the reputation of the company. Mortgages, on the other hand, are guaranteed by the value of the mortgaged property.

accumulated

Paragraph 8

After a company subtracts its debts from its assets, the figure arrived at is the net worth of the company or its owners' equity. Depending upon the type of company, there are different types of owners. A corporation is owned by stockholders, and so equity will be shown as the value of the stock. This value is the book value. It may or may not be equal to the value of the stock on the stock exchange or market value. Companies whose stock is selling at prices considerably below book value are likely to be taken over by other companies. The owners' equity of a partnership is allocated according to the articles of co-partnership. For a sole proprietor, there is only one owner and the owner's equity is the value of the business to him.

An example of a balance sheet for a privately held corporation.

HARRIS LUMBER COMPANY
Statement of Financial Condition
as of December 31, 1965

ASSETS

Current Assets

Cash:			
Cash on Hand	$ 944.96		
United California Bank	4,915.82		
		$ 5,860.78	
Notes Receivable		1,327.20	
Accounts Receivable		18,576.59	
Inventory		45,683.71	
Prepaid Insurance		1,068.29	
Prepaid Expense		7.50	
	Total Current Assets		$ 72,524.07

Fixed Assets

Machinery & Equipment	$ 7,789.47		
Less: Accumulated Depr.	2,900.86		
		$ 4,888.61	
Truck & Automobile	$ 7,934.91		
Less: Accumulated Depr.	5,784.16		
		2,150.75	
Furniture & Fixtures	$ 1,382.85		
Less: Accumulated Depr.	697.10		
		685.75	
	Total Fixed Assets		7,725.11

Other Assets

Incorporation Expense		225.00
	TOTAL ASSETS	**$ 80,474.18**

HARRIS LUMBER COMPANY
Statement of Financial Condition
as of December 31, 1965

LIABILITIES & CAPITAL*

Current Liabilities

Accounts Payable	$ 9,608.97	
Accrued Wages	73.26	
Accrued Sales Tax	1,218.36	
Accrued Payroll Taxes	851.83	
Accrued Transportation Tax	2.07	
Accrued Rent	1,144.51	
Customers Deposits	20.00	
Total Current Liabilities		$ 12,919.00

Long Term Liabilities

Notes Payable	28,573.61	
Total Liabilities		$ 41,492.61

Capital*

Capital Stock Authorized & Issued	$ 5,000.00	
Retained Earnings 1/1/65	$ 24,519.75	
Less: Distributions	1,983.23	
	22,536.52	
Net Profit for Year Ending December 31, 1965	11,445.05	
Retained Earnings 12/31/65	33,981.57	
Total Capital		38,981.57
TOTAL LIABILITIES & CAPITAL		$ 80,474.18

*In this example owners' equity is referred to as capital.

Vocabulary Building Introduction

A: Vocabulary in context

Each of the following groups of sentences contains a similar idea expressed in a different way. Try to determine the meanings of the italicized words and expressions.

1. The business *transactions* are first recorded in the journal. The bookkeeper records sales and purchases in the *journal*. The *journal* is the book of original entry.

2. The bookkeeper *transfers* figures from the journal to the *ledger*. The bookkeeper *posts* the journal figures in the *book containing all the accounts*.

3. The sales transactions are posted in the sales *account*. Cash received is posted in the cash *account*. *Accounts* are records of similar types of transactions.

4. *Bookkeeping* involves recording *sales and expenditures* in the journal and posting them to the ledger. *Bookkeepers* record the *financial transactions*.

5. *Accounting* is more sophisticated than bookkeeping. *Accountants* design bookkeeping and accounting systems. Accountants *construct* financial statements.

6. Accountants *interpret* financial statements. Accountants can *tell what* financial statements *mean*.

7. Managers use financial statements *when deciding* how to *invest their capital*. Managers use the information in financial statements as a *basis* for *allocating financial resources*.

8. We can calculate *how much income tax we must pay* by looking at our financial statements. Financial statements are used for determining *income tax liabilities*.

9. The totals on the left side of the sheet *are equal to* the totals on the right side of the sheet. The *balance sheet* shows that the Assets = Liabilities + Owners' Equity. The totals are in *balance*.

10. Each item on the left side indicates *something which the company owns*. The *assets* are itemized on the left side of the balance sheet.

11. We will receive this *payment* during the *present* business year. *Accounts receivable* are listed as *current* assets.

12. The company will sell this *merchandise this year*. Inventories are also carried on the books as *current* assets.

13. If the company needs some additional cash, they can *sell* some of the *securities* that they own. *Stocks and bonds* are easy to *liquidate.*

14. We expect to use this new equipment for five years. We can *depreciate* this machinery over the next five years. After five years this machinery will have no value to the company. We will *expense twenty percent of its cost* each year.

15. Furniture, *fixtures,* and buildings are fixed assets. *Fixed assets* generally cannot be moved. A building in which there is a restaurant has *lights, stoves, and sinks.* This equipment is attached to the building.

16. The right side of the balance sheet *lists debts* which the company owes. The *liabilities are itemized* on the right side of the balance sheet.

17. Companies owe *money* to banks who have lent them money. They must pay this money back *this year.* Creditors have supplied the company with *short term* money. These are *current liabilities.*

18. They have not *paid their employees* for the past two weeks' work. *Accrued wages* payable is another current liability.

19. They *owe money* to companies who have sold them supplies. These suppliers *must be paid within ninety days.* Current liabilities include *accounts payable.*

20. The money borrowed for purchasing the building can be paid over the *next thirty years. Mortgages* are regarded as *long term liabilities.*

21. *Utility companies* issue bonds *to finance expansion projects.* The electric *company* sold securities in order *to obtain capital for building an additional generator.*

22. Investors are willing to purchase bonds issued by this company based on its *good reputation.* It's a *well-known* company and analysis of its balance sheet reveals it to be in sound *financial condition.*

23. Subtracting the *debts from the assets* reveals the *equity* of the company. The *net worth* of a company is its *value to its owners.*

24. This stock is trading at well below *book value.* Maybe a larger company with a lot of cash will *offer to purchase the outstanding shares.* The *net worth divided by the number of outstanding shares of stock* is much higher than the *market value* of the stock. This company may be *taken over* by a larger company.

25. If the airline doesn't pay back the *money it borrowed* to purchase the new *aircraft,* the bank can take the aircraft to *settle the debt.* The *mortgages* are guaranteed by the value of the *secured property.*

B: Matching

Match the words and phrases which have similar meanings.

1. transactions   _____ a . the purchase of one company by another

2. transfer to the ledger   _____ b . assets minus liabilities

3. ledger   _____ c . money owed to the company

4. accounts   _____ d . securities sold by the electric company

5. income tax liability   _____ e . sales and expenditures, for example

6. asset   _____ f . long term money

7. receivable   _____ g . book of accounts

8. present   _____ h . cost of a share on the exchange

9. inventory   _____ i . records of similar transactions

10. liquidate   _____ j . something of value

11. fixed asset   _____ k . property which guarantees a mortgage

12. list   _____ l . post

13. thirty year mortgage   _____ m. tax which must be paid

14. utility bonds   _____ n . net worth divided by number of outstanding shares

15. finance   _____ o . current

16. net worth   _____ p . merchandise

17. book value   _____ q . obtain capital

18. market value   _____ r . itemize

19. secured property _____ s . sell for cash

20. take over   _____ t . a building, for example

C: Multiple choice

This exercise is designed to increase vocabulary and reading comprehension. Select the answer which best completes the meaning of the sentence or explains the meaning of the sentence.

1. Financial information is regularly transferred from the journal to a book containing all the accounts. This means that the figures are
   a. Entered in the journal.
   b. Balanced.
   c. Posted in the ledger.
   d. Considered as assets.

2. The best way to explain the difference between bookkeeping and accounting is
   a. Bookkeeping is done by a bookkeeper, but accounting must be done by an accountant.
   b. Bookkeeping is the daily recording of financial information, but accounting is the design and maintenance of the bookkeeping system.
   c. Bookkeeping is done in the journal, but accounting is done in the ledger.
   d. Bookkeeping is more sophisticated than accounting.

3. An accountant can interpret the information found in the ledger and use it to construct financial statements. This means an accountant can
   a. Make financial decisions for the company.
   b. Allocate capital resources.
   c. Prepare a balance sheet and income-expense statement after examining the accounts.
   d. Analyze bookkeeping procedures.

4. Management analyzes the financial statements and uses them as a basis for allocating financial resources. This means
   a. All transactions and sales of securities must be considered.
   b. The statements help them decide how to invest their capital.
   c. The sale of securities can help finance expansion.
   d. All of the above.

5. Banks and insurance companies often invest their capital in securities.
   a. They purchase stocks and bonds which they hope will increase in value and which pay dividends or interest.
   b. They want to be sure that their debtors will pay them back.
   c. This increases the value of their assets and decreases the value of their equity.
   d. None of the above.

6. In one of the following ways, the tax laws indicate how the fixed assets are to be depreciated:
   a. You should subtract a certain portion of the cost based on how long you will use the equipment.

b. The value of the land declines by twenty percent each year.
c. In order to determine the tax liabilities, you must use the formula specified by the tax law.
d. The decline in value of the building cannot be determined from the tax formula.

7. Since all the fixtures are included in the price of the building,
   a. Lighting and plumbing equipment are to be removed by the seller.
   b. All attached shelves and heating equipment must show a decline in value.
   c. Air conditioning and other attached electrical and plumbing devices will remain attached when the building is sold.
   d. All of the above.

8. Money which the bank lent us to finance inventory and accounts receivable must be paid back this year.
   a. Short term money is regarded as a current liability.
   b. We can repay this debt as our customers pay us what they owe.
   c. The merchandise we have for sale was used to secure this loan.
   d. All of the above.

9. Employees were not paid during the week when we prepared the balance sheet.
   a. Accrued wages are a long term liability.
   b. Accrued wages are a current asset.
   c. The money we owe the employees should be listed as a current liability.
   d. The employees are paid only twice a month.

10. Because the company is in good financial condition, it will be able to sell bonds to finance construction of additional production equipment.
    a. The repayment of the bonds will be secured by the value of the new equipment.
    b. The bond purchasers will hold a mortgage on the new equipment.
    c. Investors in the bonds believe the company has a good reputation.
    d. Long-term money must be secured.

Listening and Note-Taking Skills

This lesson concerns the activities of bookkeeping and accounting, and the preparation of the balance sheet. Basically, there are three methods used to present the material. They are definition of terms, description of items and their arrangement on the financial statement, and the reasons for and uses of procedures and records. In previous chapters, we have listed words and phrases which indicate definitions, such as *means, refers to, is considered.* We have also discussed the use of examples to illustrate meanings and to describe. In this lesson listen for words indicating position and arrangement such as *on the right, listed.* The reasons for certain procedures and activities are indicated by words such as *used for, used to, as a basis, determine.*

D: Comprehension questions

Listen to Paragraphs 1, 2, 3, and 4 and answer the following questions concerning definitions, descriptions, and reasons.

1. Why do businesses keep financial records?
2. Where are business transactions first recorded?
3. What is another name for the journal?
4. What are examples of things recorded in the journal?
5. What word means transferring figures from the journal to the ledger?
6. What is contained in the ledger?
7. What do we call a record of similar financial transactions?
8. What is the name for the activity of designing, maintaining, and interpreting financial information?
9. What do accountants do with the information contained in the accounts?
10. Why do managers need financial statements?
11. What does the balance sheet indicate?
12. Why is it called a balance sheet?
13. Where are the assets itemized?
14. What is another word for owners' equity?
15. What are two kinds of assets?
16. How are current assets defined?

E: Outlining

Write an outline of Paragraphs 1–4.

F: Completing an outline

The topics for Paragraphs 5, 6, 7, and 8 are listed below. Listen to these paragraphs and complete the outline indicating your own divisions and subdivisions. Notice that liabilities are in categories similar to assets.

Owners' equity is discussed according to the legal form of organization of the business.

V. A. Fixed Assets (1. Definition; 2. Examples)
   B. Value Less Depreciation (1. Definition; 2. Example)
VI. Other Fixed Assets
VII. Liabilities
VIII. Owners' Equity

Reading Comprehension

G: Comprehension questions

Paragraphs 1, 2, and 3 of this lesson are introductory. They discuss the need for bookkeeping and accounting, and how bookkeeping and accounting information is used to construct a balance sheet indicating the financial condition of a business. The remaining paragraphs describe the various sections of the balance sheet and what they show. The balance sheet is really a classification of financial information: similar items are grouped together, and their similarity is explained. Answer the following questions about the balance sheet based on your reading of Paragraphs 4, 5, 6, 7, and 8.

1. Why is merchandise regarded as a current asset?
2. What do companies often do with extra cash?
3. What effect do slow sales have on liquidity?
4. How would machinery and production equipment be listed on the balance sheet?
5. What is one method of determining yearly depreciation of equipment?
6. How can the income tax law affect figures on the balance sheet?
7. What is the difference between calculating the value of land and the value of a building?
8. What is similar between the classification of liabilities and the classification of assets?
9. Where do companies list debts on which they must pay interest?
10. Where do they list the interest they must pay?
11. What is the main difference between a bond and a mortgage?
12. What is a similarity between a bond and a mortgage?
13. How does a company determine its net worth?

14. What is the book value of a stock?

15. Why would a company want to take over another company whose stock was trading at much less than its book value?

Writing

The portion of this lesson describing the balance sheet is written in a method that organizes information. We refer to this method as classification. Just as the account groups together similar financial transactions, the balance sheet groups together similar accounts. Another method of organizing information is called comparison and contrast. If items have some similar characteristics we can compare them; if they have opposite characteristics we can contrast them. If two items are exactly alike, there is no need to compare them. We would simply say that they are exactly alike. On the other hand, if two things are completely different, having no common characteristics or uses, there is no point in contrasting them. The balance sheet provides us with several items which, although they share certain characteristics, in some ways are also different. For example, current assets are both similar to and different from current liabilities. Fixed assets are similar to and different from long-term liabilities. An understanding of these similarities and differences will help us to understand why these items have been placed in their respective categories on the balance sheet.

H: Writing a paragraph

Write a paragraph in which you discuss the similarities and differences between current assets and liabilities or fixed assets and long-term liabilities. First make a list of the similarities between the two groups, and then make a list of the differences. Your conclusion should state that as a result of these similarities and differences, a balance sheet is able to express these characteristics in graphic form.

Vocabulary Review: Rephrasing

I: Rephrasing words and expressions

Rewrite the following sentences. Replace the words and expressions in italics with expressions from the text which have the same meaning.

1. All businesses need to *record financial transactions* in order to know whether or not they are *profitable*.

2. In daily business operations figures are first entered in the *book of original entry*.

3. Periodically, bookkeepers *post journal figures* in the book containing all the accounts of the company.

4. Accountants use *ledger information* to construct *balance sheets* and *income expense statements*.

5. Management uses financial statements *in order to make* business decisions and in order to determine *how much tax to pay*.

6. The *value of the company* is equal to the *amount of money it owes to creditors* and the *amount it owes to its owners*.

7. On the right side of the *page* are listed the *debts* and the *net worth*.

8. Certain items of value to the company are *bought and sold on a regular basis*; other items are *held by the company for a long time*.

9. *Inventories* and *receivables* are considered current assets.

10. If a company needs to have cash, it can *sell* some of its securities.

11. The value of machinery is determined by subtracting its *decline in value due to use* from its original cost to the company.

12. The *formula for determining the decline in value* may be *specified* in the tax law.

13. *Equipment attached to the building* should also show *decline in value*.

14. *Debts* are divided into two groups: debts to be paid during the present business year; debts to be paid over many years.

15. This debt is *secured by an interest in* the property.

16. Investors purchasing these *securities* believe in the *good name* of the company.

Oral Practice

Debate

Resolved: Corporate balance sheets should all be computerized. It is a faster and more accurate method of record keeping, and the records cannot be dishonestly altered. That way the true financial condition of a company would be immediately apparent to all. (Discuss the arguments for and against this.)

Glossary for Lesson Nine
Financial Statements

Account: a financial record of similar transactions.

Sales transactions are recorded in the sales *account.*

Accountant: a person who has received professional training in the field of accounting.

The duty of the cost *accountant* is to try to control the costs of production.

Accounting: the design and maintenance of a system of financial records and the interpretation of the data contained in them.

Retail businesses usually use an *accounting* system different from the system used by manufacturing firms.

Accumulate: collect or total up.

If you put money in a savings account it will *accumulate* interest.

Fixed assets should indicate their original cost less the *accumulated* depreciation.

Allocate: to assign or distribute among different purposes.

The company will *allocate* a certain amount of money for research and development.

Asset: money or something of value to a company.

Most of the company's *assets* are invested in plant and equipment.

A diesel truck is an *asset* to a trucking company.

Balance sheet: a financial statement listing the assets, liabilities, and net worth of a company.

The accounting department prepares a *balance sheet* every June 30.

Bond: a security which indicates the debt of a company to the owner of the bond.

A *bond* indicates that interest will be paid at a certain rate until a future certain date when the principal will be paid.

Bonds are usually sold in denominations of $1,000 or $5,000.

In order to raise capital for expansion, the utility company is selling thirty year *bonds* which pay sixteen percent interest.

Bookkeepers: employees who record the day-to-day transactions of the company in the proper account.

Bookkeepers usually do not have as much training as accountants.

Book value: a value determined by dividing the net worth of a corporation by the number of outstanding shares of common stock.

The *book value* of the stock indicates the assets per share. It may have nothing to do with the price per share.

Current: present, up-do-date.

Because the bookkeeper has been sick, the books are not *current*.

During the *current* year, the company hopes to increase sales ten percent.

Depreciate: an accounting process which decreases the value of certain fixed assets according to their use. It allows for the firm to recover the cost of their capital over a certain period of time.

Since the airline expects to use the new jets for ten years, they can *depreciate* them ten percent per year.

Depreciation: the decrease in value of certain fixed assets due to use and wear.

The original cost of the vehicle was $10,000 and the accumulated *depreciation* is $3,000. Its value as an asset is $7,000.

Enter: to record (a financial transaction) in a journal or ledger.

These figures are *entered* on Page 43 of the journal.

Entry: a figure which has been entered in a journal or ledger.

According to the *entry* on Page 45, sales last month showed a decrease from the month before.

Expansion: growth, the increase in size of a business activity.

The company requires more capital for the *expansion* of production facilities.

Expense: money which was spent.

A traveling salesman has an *expense* account which pays him back (reimburses) for expenses such as gasoline and hotel bills.

The statement of *expenses* shows how much money the company spent in order to stay in business.

Expense (also used as a verb): to record in accounting as an expense.

We can *expense* the cost of this item since its useful life is less than one year.

Financial resources: capital which is available for use by the company.

The managers must decide how to allocate *financial resources* in the most profitable manner.

Fixed: unchanging, attached permanently.

Fixed assets are those assets which will stay with the company for a long period of time.

Fixture: equipment which is used in the business and which is attached to the building.

I asked the maintenance man to replace the light *fixture* in my office.

In a service station, the gas pumps and grease rack are regarded as *fixtures*.

Formula: a mathematical process for determining certain values.

The *formula* for determining the amount of interest due is $I = Prt$, where I is the interest, P is the principal, r is the rate of interest, and t is the time.

The *formula* for determining depreciation is part of the tax law.

Income: money which a company or individual receives in the course of doing business.

The gross *income* is all the money which the company receives.

The net *income* is the gross *income* minus the expenses.

Interpretation: the process of determining the meaning of something.

The accountants are not only responsible for the maintenance of the financial records, but also their *interpretation*.

Management *interprets* the financial statements and makes decisions about the operations of the company.

Journal: the book where financial transactions are first recorded.

The entry in the *journal* indicates the date, the accounts affected, and a brief description of the transaction.

Periodically, figures are transferred from the *journal* to the ledger.

Ledger: a book containing all the accounts for a company.

The information in the *ledger* is used to construct financial statements.

Liabilities: debts; money which the company owes to another company, a bank, or an individual.

Money which the company has borrowed from the bank is listed on the balance sheet as a *liability*.

Long term: refers to a period of usually ten years or more.

Utility companies sell *long-term* bonds in order to finance construction of new power plants.

Market or trading value: the price at which stocks are being traded on the stock exchange.

If the *market value* is much lower than the book value, a larger company may decide to offer to purchase all the outstanding shares of stock of a company and take it over.

Mortgage: a document which gives the title or ownership rights, but not possession of, a piece of property to a creditor as guarantee for the payment of a loan; also, the value of the loan.

You can purchase the building with a twenty percent down payment and a *mortgage* for the remaining eighty percent.

Mortgages are long-term liabilities.

Net worth: also referred to as owners' equity; the difference between the value of the assets of a company and the value of its liabilities.

Assets are equal to liabilities plus *net worth*.

Outstanding: not yet paid.

Your account has an *outstanding* balance of $1,204.03.

Payable: debts which must be paid during the present business cycle.

Accounts *payable* are listed as current assets.

Posting: the transferring of journal entries to the ledger.

This money will be *posted* to your account immediately.

Record: a written financial document or one that is permanently stored in some other manner such as on film or magnetic tape; also to write or store financial information.

The bookkeeper *records* all financial transactions in the journal.

The journal is a *record* of financial transactions.

Receivable: money which should be paid to a company during the present business cycle.

Accounts *receivable* are listed as current assets.

Our *receivables* are increasing since customers are slow to make their payments.

Reputation: respect, trust, and good name.

Companies that have excellent *reputations* and a sound financial condition can offer lower interest rates on their bonds than can other companies.

Statement: a financial report which usually shows totals and balances.

Every month the bank mails out *statements* of the accounts.

Take over: the purchase of an entire company by another company.

If a larger company purchases fifty-one percent of the outstanding stock of a smaller company, it will *take over* that company.

It is sometimes illegal for a company to *take over* one of its competitors.

Transaction: a business activity which involves the transfer of money, goods, and/or services.

All business *transactions* must be recorded in the journal.

Transfer: to convey or move from one place to another.

This financial information needs to be *transferred* to the ledgers.

Introduction to Lesson Ten:
International Business

International Business is included here because it is assumed that most readers of this text are involved in international trade. We begin with a discussion of the theory of international trade and then deal with the reactions of governments and multinational businesses to the opportunities and problems presented by this trade.

Vocabulary in this lesson includes terms related to geography, government regulations, import and export, and international financing and banking. Vocabulary exercise A deals with synonyms and definitions, and vocabulary exercise B deals with understanding concepts and ideas as well as making inferences.

Listening exercise C can be answered with short answers as students listen to passages being read, or it could be done as a reading exercise and answered with complete sentences. The reading comprehension questions, exercise E, generally require longer answers and some interpretation of the text.

The writing exercise in this lesson requires the student to use imagination and to organize events into chronological order. This exercise could also be used as an oral presentation or even as a topic for a panel discussion to emphasize conversational skills.

Linguistic concepts useful for this lesson are abbreviations and derivations, suffixes, adverbs of time, and adverbial phrases and clauses.

Coca Cola is an example of a multinational company whose products are produced and sold world wide. Here is a bottle of coke produced in the People's Republic of China.

10

International Business

Basic Factors and Ideas in International Business

Paragraph 1

Most countries realize the advantages of world trade. Countries have developed their economies, increased production of goods, and met market demands through increased world trade. The interdependence among trading nations has provided increased business opportunities.

Paragraph 2

International trade develops because certain countries are able to produce some goods more efficiently than other countries. They exchange goods to satisfy their needs and wants. Efficient production may be the result of several factors. A certain climate in a particular country may allow that country to grow agricultural products in abundance. For instance, the climates in the United States and Canada are suitable for production of large amounts of wheat. Natural resources such as oil or coal are abundant in other countries. Countries with a large pool of

requiring a
lot of labor

deal in

unskilled laborers are able to produce products which are <u>labor inten-sive</u> more cheaply than countries with highly paid, skilled labor forces. Another factor is geographical location. Countries like Singapore and Panama <u>engage in</u> banking and trading because they are located on world trade routes.

Paragraph 3

believed

The Scottish economist, Adam Smith (1723–1790), <u>theorized</u> that in a free market countries produce whatever they can most efficiently grow or manufacture, or what is of the greatest advantage to them. In other words, if they can make more money growing cotton than making cloth, they grow cotton and export it. Then they import cloth from a country that makes cloth more efficiently than it grows cotton. In an uncon-trolled free market trade situation, there is international <u>specialization</u> which results in the most efficient production of goods. Therefore, competition guarantees that countries import products which are most efficiently manufactured <u>abroad</u> and export products which are most efficiently produced <u>domestically</u>. Price is determined by the <u>supply side of the market</u>. Smith's theory was a theory of absolute advantage. The English economist, David Ricardo (1772–1823), refined Smith's theory to one of comparative advantage. He theorized that an exporting country does not have to be the most efficient producer of the product; it only has to be more efficient than the country which imports the product. <u>Mutually beneficial trade</u> arises when one country has a comparative advantage.

division of labor

in other countries
at home; quantity
available for sale

a basis for trade
which benefits
both countries

Paragraph 4

There are several reasons why governments try to control the imports and exports of a country. One reason is that a country enjoys an advantage if it exports more than it imports. Wealth accrues to the exporting country. Some countries have special programs to encourage exports. They may be programs that provide marketing information, establish trade missions, subsidize exports, and <u>provide tax benefits or incentives</u>. Government <u>subsidies</u> allow companies to sell products cheaply. Sometimes these subsidized companies export their products and sell them cheaply <u>overseas</u>. This practice is known as dumping. Dumping is selling on a foreign market at a price below the cost of production.

reduce taxes
financial support

in foreign countries

Paragraph 5

limit

On the other hand, governments impose taxes and quotas to <u>restrict</u> imports of certain products. For example, to protect Japanese farmers,

Japan limits the amount of produce that can be imported. Sometimes governments want to protect a domestic industry because that industry provides employment for the population. Not only the industries, but also the labor unions encourage the government to <u>enact</u> protectionist controls.

establish

Paragraph 6

laws/controls; taxes

Protectionist <u>measures</u> are in the form of <u>duties</u> which eliminate the comparative advantage, or quotas which restrict the import of the product altogether. There are two forms of import <u>tariffs</u>: specific and *ad valorem*. A specific tariff is a certain amount of tax for each unit of the product, for example $500 for each automobile. An *ad valorem* tariff is based on the value of the product, for example 5% of its value. Thus, under an *ad valorem* tax a Rolls Royce imported to the United States would be taxed more than a Datsun. The <u>imposition</u> of the *ad valorem* tax depends upon first determining the value of the product. The United States uses the free on board (FOB) method, which is the cost of the product as it leaves the exporting country. European countries have adopted the cost insurance freight (CIF) method, which adds the value of place utility to the cost of the product. A tariff increases the price of the item, raises revenue for the government, and controls consumption through market forces. A quota has a different effect on the market because it limits the number of items imported. While under a quota there may be a higher price because of a limited supply, under a tariff it is the tax that creates a higher price: the supply is not limited.

taxes

levying

Paragraph 7

In order to import and export products, there needs to be a system of international monetary exchange. While a few products like oil are always priced in dollars, most products must be paid for with the <u>legal</u> <u>tender</u> of the producing country. International trade involves the exchange of one currency for another. Most currencies are now exchanged on a <u>floating</u> rate basis. There are no official exchange rates. The rates <u>fluctuate</u> according to market forces. If large amounts of a country's currency are being exchanged, the exchange rate may vary greatly because demand, and therefore, the price of a currency is either rising or falling. Sometimes these great fluctuations in value threaten economic stability; then central banks change market forces by purchasing a foreign currency to support its price and maintain stability.

currency

variable
change

Paragraph 8

The amount of money that goes in and out of a country is referred to as the balance of payments. If a country is exporting more than it imports, it is receiving foreign currency and has a balance of trade surplus. If it is importing more than it exports, it is sending money out of the country and has a balance of trade deficit. Continued surpluses or deficits change the demand for the currency of a country and cause its value to float either upward or downward.

Paragraph 9

The comparative advantage which exporting countries enjoy sometimes changes. If transportation costs increase or currency exchange rates change, it may become cheaper to produce the product in the market country, especially if large amounts of exports are involved.

Paragraph 10

branch companies Exporting companies sometimes set up <u>subsidiaries</u> in the market countries. The larger company is referred to as the parent company. Some countries have laws restricting the foreign ownership of factories or other production facilities, while others encourage foreign investment. A large company that sets up production facilities in several different countries is referred to as a multinational. Multinational corporations **world wide** develop a <u>global</u> philosophy of management, marketing, and produc-**provide** tion. They choose to operate in those countries that <u>afford</u> them comparative advantages.

Vocabulary Building Introduction

A: Vocabulary in context

Read the following sentences carefully and pay particular attention to the words in *italics*.

1. Most countries today realize the *advantages* of world trade. Most countries *benefit* from world trade. World trade provides economic development and increased business opportunities.

2. Countries with many unskilled laborers are able to produce *labor-intensive* products efficiently. *Large pools* of unskilled workers are needed to make things which require a lot of hand labor. Electronic devices are *assembled* where labor is inexpensive.

3. *Geographical* location can be a *benefit* if a country is engaged in *international trade*. Some countries have an advantage in the *import* and *export* business because of their location.

4. In a *free market* situation producers can purchase their raw materials and sell their finished products without being *restricted* by government regulations. When there is *free trade*, there are no *tariffs* and quotas.

5. An international *division of labor* results in the *most efficient* production of goods. If the workers in each country *specialize in what they do best*, manufacturing *costs will be less*.

6. *High volume* production results in lower costs. The price is determined by the *supply side* of the market.

7. Countries *import* products which are not produced *domestically*. We can purchase these products cheaply *overseas*.

8. The sales manager would like to know if we can market these products *abroad*. If there is demand *in other countries*, we will begin to export this product.

9. The United States enjoys an advantage in the production of food compared to Japan. Japan has a *comparative advantage* in the production of motorcycles. Trade between the two countries will benefit both of them. This *mutually beneficial* trade is the result of each country's comparative advantage.

10. Countries that export more than they import *become rich. Wealth accrues* to the exporting country.

11. Government programs help companies export by establishing *trade missions*. Companies are encouraged to export, and the government *assists* them.

12. *Nationalized* industries like British Steel and Renault receive *subsidies* from governments. *Government owned* industries receive *financial support* from the government.

13. U.S. Steel accused British Steel of *dumping* because steel was being sold in the United States at lower prices than in Great Britain.

14. Governments sometimes *protect* domestic industries from foreign competition. Trade restrictions and *import duties* are forms of *protectionism*. Trade *restrictions* were imposed because foreign *dumping* was resulting in high unemployment among workers in the steel industry.

15. There is an *ad valorem* import tax of 6%. The duty is equal to 6% of the value of the item.

16. The *tariff* on alcohol is $2 per liter of spirits and $1 per liter of wine. The cost of the wine or spirits does not matter; this is a *specific tax*.

17. The government is *restricting* the import of fresh meat to one hundred tons. No amounts in excess of the *quota* may be imported.

18. The *legal tender* in the Federal Republic of Germany is the deutsche mark (DM). Producers in Japan want to be paid in yen (Y). The dollars ($) must be *exchanged* for yen or marks.

19. Currencies are now being exchanged on a *floating rate basis.* The exchange rate *changes* according to supply and demand for the *currency.* The rates *fluctuate* according to *market forces.*

20. Large numbers of people were *converting* dollars to *deutsche marks* and the German government *began purchasing dollars* in order to *stabilize* its value. The central bank in Germany *supported the value* of the dollar.

21. The United States imported more goods last month than it exported. The balance of *trade deficit* was $1.2 billion. Japan exports more than it imports. It always enjoys a balance of *trade surplus.*

22. Honda of America is an American *branch* of the Japanese firm. The *parent company* in Japan set up this *subsidiary* to produce motorcycles in the United States.

23. *Multinational* corporations have a *worldwide* philosophy of management and marketing. Their *global* strategy is to operate and produce in many countries so that they enjoy each country's comparative advantage.

B: Matching

Match the words in the left column with phrases in the right column that have the same meaning.

1. advantage — a . a company with a worldwide management and production philosophy

2. labor pool — b . excess of imports over exports

3. free market — c . company which owns a subsidiary

4. division of labor — d . foreign

5. overseas — e . beneficial condition

6. domestic — f . without government restrictions regulating trade

7. floating rate — g . worldwide

8. subsidy — h . group of workers

9. protectionism — i . home

10. dumping — j . tariff based on value

11. tariff — k . limit

12. *ad valorem* tax _____ l . trade restrictions to benefit domestic producers

13. specific tax _____ m. below cost foreign sale

14. quota _____ n . labor specialization

15. currency _____ o . money given to cover losses and assist nonprofit enterprises

16. exchange _____ p . cost plus insurance plus freight

17. legal tender _____ q . money value not determined by gold or a fixed standard

18. balance of trade deficit _____ r . circulating money

19. subsidiary _____ s . e.g., the dollar in the U.S., the yen in Japan

20. global _____ t . branch company

21. multinational _____ u . duty or tax

22. parent company _____ v . unit or item tax

23. market forces _____ w. supply and demand

24. CIF _____ x . convert

C: Rephrasing ideas

This exercise is designed to increase vocabulary and reading comprehension. Select the answer which is consistent with the meaning of the sentence.

1. International trade develops because certain countries are able to produce some goods more efficiently than other countries. They exchange these goods in order to satisfy their needs and wants.
   a. Countries import the goods which they produce efficiently.
   b. Countries probably export the goods which are not efficiently produced.
   c. Countries probably exchange goods which they produce efficiently for goods which other countries produce efficiently.
   d. Efficient exchange results from international trade.

2. A certain climate in a particular country may allow that country to grow agricultural products in abundance.
   a. This country probably has a comparative advantage in agriculture.

    b. This country most likely exports farm products.

    c. This country can grow food efficiently.

    d. All of the above.

3. In an uncontrolled free market trade situation, there would be an international division of labor resulting in the most efficient production of goods.

    a. With trade restrictions, countries specialize in what they produce.

    b. The most efficient production is a result of a free market.

    c. Specialization in production should be left uncontrolled.

    d. Labor always favors a free market trade situation.

4. Price is determined by the supply side of the market.

    a. If the demand for products increased so would the price.

    b. There is such an abundance of products for sale that prices would have to increase.

    c. If the supply is low, the price is low.

    d. Supply is more of a factor than demand in determining the price.

5. A basis for mutually beneficial trade is the fact that one country has a comparative advantage.

    a. Both the importing country and the exporting country benefit from trade.

    b. One country's comparative advantage can benefit another country.

    c. The comparative advantage of one country can result in trade between countries.

    d. All of the above.

6. A country can accrue wealth if it exports more than it imports.

    a. This country has a balance of trade deficit.

    b. Demand for this country's currency will fall.

    c. This country receives money from countries which import its products.

    d. All of the above.

7. Governments try to control imports of products to protect domestic industries.

    a. Protectionist measures take the form of import duties and quotas.

    b. Protectionist measures insure free trade.

    c. Workers are always opposed to protectionism.

    d. All protectionist policies have the same effect on the market.

8. Selling products abroad at prices lower than the cost of production is known as *dumping*.

    a. Dumping is always against government policy.

b. Dumping is always beneficial to the importing country because buyers pay lower prices.

c. Exporters dump products on foreign markets to lower domestic employment.

d. Some reasons for dumping could be inventory reduction, maintenance of domestic employment, and continuation of high production levels.

9. Most currencies are now exchanged on a floating rate basis in which there are no official exchange rates, and rates fluctuate according to market forces.

a. If money changers want to sell dollars for yen, the price of the dollar will decline.

b. An exporting country with a balance of payments surplus may accumulate a lot of foreign currency for which demand is low, thus making their exports more expensive.

c. The supply and demand for currencies determine the exchange rates.

d. All of the above.

10. Multinational companies set up production facilities in countries where production is most efficient.

a. All countries allow foreign ownership of production facilities.

b. The larger company is called the parent company; the production facilities are referred to as a subsidiary.

c. Subsidiary companies eliminate the problem of worldwide competition.

d. Each subsidiary needs to consider only local market conditions.

Listening and Note-Taking Skills

D: Comprehension questions

Listen to the passage and answer the following questions about Paragraphs 1, 2, 3, 4, and 5.

1. What advantages do countries derive from world trade?

2. How does efficient production give rise to world trade?

3. How could climate affect a country's production efficiency?

4. How could unskilled laborers be an advantage to a country?

5. How does a free market system determine where goods should be produced?

6. According to Ricardo, what situation would result in mutually beneficial trade?

7. Why do governments encourage exports?

8. How do governments encourage exports?

9. Why do governments try to control imports?

10. What groups sometimes encourage protectionism?

Reading and Note-Taking Skills

E: Completing an outline

Write an outline of the reading using the following headings and beginning with Paragraph 1. (The Roman numerals do not refer to the paragraph numbers.)

I. Advantages of World Trade

II. Production Efficiency and World Trade

III. Two Theories Regarding International Trade (A. Adam Smith's theory; B. David Ricardo's theory)

IV. Government Policies (A. Encouragement of exports; B. Control of imports)

V. International Monetary Exchange (A. Exchange rates; B. Balance of payments)

VI. Multinational Companies (A. Creation; B. Methods of operation)

Reading Comprehension

F: Comprehension questions

This lesson discusses four aspects of international business. The first deals with the reasons for the existence of international trade and how it is a logical response to the free market. The second section deals with government regulation of this free market. Next, the lesson discusses the present method of monetary exchange made necessary by the control governments exert over currencies. Finally, the concept of a multinational corporation is derived as a response to the effects of the other three factors. International business is a dynamic activity which changes, adapts, and responds according to conditions. When answering the following questions, it is sometimes necessary to infer an answer. The answers to some of these questions are not expressly stated in the text. Just as international business is an outgrowth of and a response to business entrepreneurship, your answers may be an outgrowth of your reading and thinking about the text.

1. How might underdeveloped countries benefit from international trade?
2. What types of business opportunities are presented as a result of interdependence among trading nations?
3. What four factors mentioned would contribute to a country's production efficiency?
4. According to the text, what is the main difference between Smith's theory and Ricardo's theory?
5. Explain how exporting countries become wealthy.
6. Why would a country object to foreign countries dumping goods?
7. Why might a government subsidize an inefficient export industry?
8. What are two forms of protectionism?
9. What is one advantage of tariffs over quotas to a government?
10. Why do tariffs and quotas have different effects on the market?
11. With a floating exchange rate, what would happen to the exchange value of currency from a country that exports more than it imports?
12. Explain why the value of the currency of a country that imports more than it exports would tend to decrease.
13. What would be a good reason for an exporting company to set up a subsidiary in the country that imports its product?
14. What is a parent company?
15. Why might a country encourage foreign investment or the establishment of subsidiaries of foreign companies?

Writing

A scenario is a description of imagined events. We sometimes use a scenario to describe what could happen or what might have happened. A scenario is a useful management tool because we can use it to describe what would be the result of a management decision. For example, what would be the result of increased promotional activities? Sales would increase and we would have to develop new distribution plans to get the products to the consumers. If sales increased beyond a certain amount, it might be necessary to build new production facilities closer to the markets. The elements of the scenario are in chronological order. That is, the events are described in the order in which they would occur.

G: Writing a business scenario

Write a scenario or description of events about a company that decides to export a certain product to another country. Describe the activities of the exporting country to encourage exports, and the reaction of the country importing the products to protect its domestic industries. What happens to the exchange rates between the two countries? The order for the events of your scenario can be the same as the order of discussion in the text. First describe the reasons for exporting; then describe the reactions of the governments and the effects on the exchange rates; and conclude with the establishment of a subsidiary.

Vocabulary Review: Rephrasing

H: Rephrasing words and expressions

Rewrite the following sentences. Replace the words and expressions in *italics* with expressions from the text which have the same meaning.

1. Most countries today *benefit from* world trade.
2. *Workers with very little training* are able to produce goods which *require a lot of hand work.*
3. Adam Smith *suggested* that in a market *without government interference* countries would produce what had the greatest advantage to them.
4. In a free market *different work would be performed in different countries.*
5. Countries *sell abroad* the goods produced most efficiently *at home.*
6. Governments try to *regulate* the imports and exports of a country.
7. Some governments *give money* to companies that export.
8. Governments try to protect their *home* industries.
9. Governments can *limit* imports by *imposing* an import *tax.*
10. An *import duty* raises *money* for the government.
11. Most goods must be paid for in the *currency* of the producing country.
12. Currencies are *bought and sold* on a floating rate basis.
13. The rates *vary* according to *market forces.*
14. *When a country is receiving foreign currency,* it means that it is exporting more than it imports.
15. The *main* company opened up a *branch* in the foreign country.
16. Multinational companies have a *worldwide* philosophy of management.

Oral Practice

Debate

Resolved: Free trade is the most advantageous system for world economy. Therefore, completely free trade is best for every individual country, no matter what the cost may be to particular industries. (Discuss the arguments for and against this.)

Glossary for Lesson Ten
International Business

Abroad: in a foreign country, overseas.

We hope to sell our new product both in the United States and *abroad.*

If you are traveling *abroad,* you need a passport.

Accrue: to accumulate, to collect.

Interest of 10% per annum *accrues* on amounts deposited in a savings account.

Ad valorem: (Latin) according to the value.

Most sales taxes are *ad valorem* taxes. They are based on the value of the item sold. For example, 6% of the value of the item is added to the cost.

Advantage: a circumstance or situation which provides a benefit.

Because of favorable weather conditions, California has an *advantage* in the production of fruits and vegetables.

Balance of payments also **balance of trade:** the difference between the value of exports and the value of imports.

Japan has a *balance of payments* surplus because it exports more than it imports.

Currency: the money in circulation, legal tender.

Importers and exporters must exchange their *currency* for the *currency* of the country with which they are doing business.

Deficit: an excess of expenses or debits over income or credits.

A country that imports more than it exports has a balance of trade *deficit.*

Devaluation: an official reduction in the exchange rates between the currencies of two countries.

The British Pound Sterling was formerly worth $3.20 (U.S.). After *devaluation* it was worth only $2.80 (U.S.).

Because of floating exchange rates, there is not a great need for currency *devaluations*. Supply and demand determine the exchange rates.

Division of labor: a situation in which one group of workers performs one type of work, and another group performs another type.

An international *division of labor* occurs when one country concentrates its labor force on the production of items it most efficiently produces with the intention of trading them for items which are most efficiently produced in another country.

Dumping: the selling of products in foreign countries at prices below those charged in the producing country, or at prices below the actual cost of production.

American steel companies accused government-subsidized British Steel of *dumping* steel on the United States market.

Duty: an import tax or tariff.

Foreign travelers will have to pay a *duty* on some items purchased abroad.

The *duty* imposed on imported products raises their prices.

E.G. (*exempli gratia*): a Latin abbreviation that is used in English to mean *for example.*

Some countries export small cars, *e.g.*, Japan.

Exchange: to trade one thing for another; here, to trade one country's currency for that of another.

I need to *exchange* these dollars for *deutsche marks.*

Export: to send a product to another country for the purpose of sale; also, the product sent.

Japan *exports* automobiles to the United States.

They produce many models just for *export.*

Free market: buying and selling activity unrestricted by government price regulation.

There is now a *free market* for clothing in the United States. The price is not controlled by the government.

Geographical: according to its location on the earth.

Singapore has an advantage in international trade because of its *geographical* location.

Global: worldwide, considering the entire world.

International trade companies need to be able to compete on a *global* basis rather than a regional basis.

A *global* communications system was made possible by satellites.

Import: to bring into a country for the purpose of sale; also, the item brought in.

Japan needs to *import* most of its raw materials.

In the United States, Japanese cars are referred to as *imports*.

Interdependence: the reliance (of countries) on one another.

Interdependence has developed among trading nations. The United States is dependent on others for oil imports and other nations are dependent upon the U.S. for food exports.

Labor intensive: refers to the use of hand labor to a greater extent than the use of raw materials or capital for the production of an item.

The clothing industry is very *labor intensive*. It takes a lot of manual labor to sew clothes.

Legal tender: the official currency of a country.

The dollar is *legal tender* in the United States. A debtor can use dollars to pay any debts, and creditors must accept them for payment.

Multinational: a company that conducts business in several countries and has a global philosophy of management.

Many developing countries encourage *multinational* companies to build production facilities.

Unilever is an important *multinational* corporation which produces and sells products in many countries.

Nationalized: taken over, controlled, and owned by the government of a country.

British Steel is a *nationalized* company because it is owned by the British government.

The socialist government in France *nationalized* all the large banks.

Parent company: a large company which owns smaller companies or subsidiaries.

International Telephone and Telegraph (I.T.T.) is a *parent company* which owns many smaller companies in the United States and abroad.

Protectionism: the enactment of laws regulating imports for the purpose of protecting domestic companies from foreign competition.

Protectionism is a barrier to foreign trade.

Quota: a limit or maximum number of items which the government will allow to be imported.

The government established a *quota* for imported beef in order to protect the domestic beef producers.

Subsidiary: a company owned by a parent company.

Ford produces parts for its automobiles at several of its foreign *subsidiaries.*

Subsidize: to assist a private company with government funds.

In many countries the governments *subsidize* the farmers in order to insure that enough food is produced.

Surplus: extra amount.

A country that exports more than it imports will have a balance of trade *surplus.*

Tariff: a tax on imports (or sometimes exports).

The new *tariffs* will make the imported products more expensive for consumers.

Theory: (verb: theorize) a general idea or framework to explain observed phenomena.

According to Adam Smith's *theory,* a free market will result in the most efficient production of goods.

Trade: to exchange one thing for another; the act of exchanging.

Foreign *trade* has resulted in benefits for the trading countries.

UAW - United Auto Workers: a labor union.

The *UAW* negotiated with General Motors for higher wages.

Unskilled: refers to manual labor requiring little training.

If a country has a large pool of *unskilled* laborers, it has an advantage in the production of labor intensive products.

Introduction to Lesson Eleven:
Computers

A lesson on computers has been included in this text for two reasons. First of all, computers are being used increasingly in modern business. (The introductory paragraph explains some of their current uses.) The second reason this lesson has been included is to present a method for the student to continue to learn new vocabulary after finishing this text. As computer technology changes, new vocabulary evolves to describe that technology. This lesson presents some of the new computer vocabulary as well as a method for approaching the evolution in terminology.

The text of the lesson begins with some definitions and then explains the different steps in the operation of a computer, the IPO (input-process-output) sequence. Next, the two major divisions are distinguished: the equipment or hardware, and the use of the equipment—the programs or software. Finally, attention is directed toward the formation of computer vocabulary. Vocabulary exercises emphasize the new vocabulary and the ways in which these words evolve, such as using initials to construct acronyms, shortening longer words to one syllable, and using words in ways grammatically different from previous usage.

The student should consider the writing exercise in this chapter as a summary of the methods of this book. The writing exercise points to the analogy between the computer and the manufacturing activity. Innovation, as it has been applied to developments in the computer field, will have an effect on all the business activities discussed in this text.

Students should learn to apply the methods of analogy to deal with computer terminology explained in this lesson as well as to understand new terminology in other areas of business. It is hoped that the techniques presented in this book have prepared the student to understand other written texts in business.

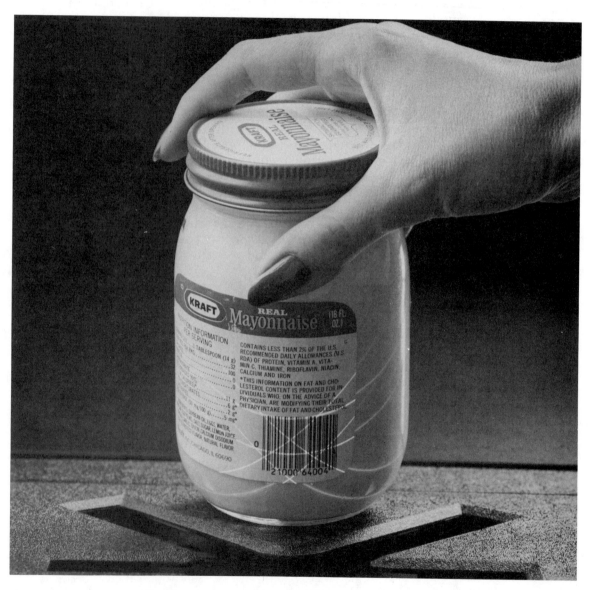

The bar coded UPC number is input to a POS minicomputer as the grocery item slides across the checkout counter.

11
Computers

Computers in Business

Paragraph 1

uses   There are as many <u>applications</u> for computers in business as there are business activities. They can be used in production to plan and coordinate materials movement, machine usage, and work schedules. In marketing and distribution they can be used to develop marketing <u>strategies</u>, process sales orders, arrange delivery schedules, and keep track of shipments on route. For managers a very important use of computers has to do with accounting and finance. Managers base many of their decisions on computer <u>generated</u> information. This lesson discusses some computer terms and concepts needed in the modern business environment and particularly the use of computers at the retail level.

plans

produced

Paragraph 2

Computers are high speed electronic machines which process data, and the use of computers is referred to as *electronic data processing* (EDP). Like most types of machines used in business, computers perform the

time consuming and repetitive work which people find generally boring.
They routinely perform operations in seconds that would require many
<u>worker hours</u> or even worker years.

work done by one worker in one hour

Paragraph 3

typewriter-like device

There are basically three steps which describe the sequence of operation
of the computer (IPO sequence). First, the data is entered. It may be
entered by means of a <u>keyboard</u>, or it may be read from a disk or
magnetic tape. Newer methods are constantly being developed. At the
retail level data is input using a laser beam and *Optical Character
Recognition* (OCR). Input data is made up of various facts or concepts
such as a certain amount of money, a certain travel destination, or a
name. Usually this data must be converted to numbers before the computer is able to process it. The *Universal Product Code* (UPC) number
on a grocery item indicates that item and its size.

Paragraph 4

Second, the data is processed. This means that the data is combined,
sorted, or acted upon according to the programmed instructions. If the
data is an amount of money, it may be added to or subtracted from
another amount of money. For example, the amount of a check is
subtracted from the balance of a checking account in a program designed for banking. In a program designed for airplane ticket reservations the destination of an airplane trip is matched to the ticket price. In
a grocery store the UPC number indicating the grocery item is matched
to the name of the product and the current price.

Paragraph 5

numbers

Third, the processed data, which is now called information, is fed out of
the computer. The information or output may be in one form or several
different ones. It may be displayed on a television screen called a *cathode
ray tube* (CRT). It may also be displayed as <u>digits</u> or letters by *light
emitting diodes* (LED's) or on a *liquid crystal display* (LCD). Output
may also be printed on paper. The bank sends us a printed statement of
our account; the airline reservation computer prints out a ticket; a cash
register computer in a grocery store presents us with an itemized receipt
of the groceries purchased.

Paragraph 6

Most products now sold at retail grocery stores are coded with the UPC.
A *point of sale* (POS) computer terminal attached to a cash register uses
a small laser beam to read the UPC number as the clerk slides the

merchandise across the counter. The POS terminal is known as a *smart* or *intelligent* terminal because it processes the data and prints out the information, in addition to serving as an input terminal to a larger central computer for the entire store. Most of the POS terminals spell out the item and its price and display them on an LED readout for the customer. The POS computers have been programmed to total the prices of all items purchased, compute the sales tax, record the sale as cash or charge, compute change owed to the customer, and print out a register tape which shows each item purchased with its cost, the total, the tax, and the change. The information about the sale is then stored or sent to the central computer to be used for other purposes such as keeping a record of merchandise sold. The information from the POS computer becomes data for the larger central computer, which uses it in a program for keeping sales records and controlling inventory.

Paragraph 7

The computer field is divided into two main parts: hardware and software. Hardware is the actual equipment used. There is input hardware such as keyboards and scanners, processing hardware (the actual computer), and output hardware such as CRT's, LED readouts, and printers. *Input* and *output* equipment (I/O equipment) is referred to as peripherals. Software is the computer program. Most computers can use several different kinds of programs. Computer programmers design programs to meet the users' needs. A UPC scanning program for use in a grocery store directs the OCR scanner to read the UPC, the processing unit to compute the correct price, and the output equipment to display the price and to print an alphabetic description of the product and its price on the customer receipt.

Paragraph 8

symbols

Modern digital computers use a binary number system. In other words, all data must be transformed into a number system consisting of only two <u>digits</u>: 0 and 1. Each 0 or 1 is referred to as a bit. (The word *bit* is contracted from *binary digit*.) All the letters of the alphabet and all of the numbers from 0 to 9 can be represented by a binary number of eight digits or eight bits. In this case, eight bits is referred to as a byte.

Paragraph 9

size

The <u>capacity</u> of a computer is indicated by the number of bytes it can store in its memory. A 64k *random access memory* (RAM) can temporarily store 64,000 bytes of information. Each byte can be read or changed in the same length of time regardless of where it is stored on the memory chip. Several types of memories exist in addition to the random access memory, such as *read only memory* (ROM) and *erasable programmable read only memory* (EPROM). The type and quantity of data to be processed and the type of processing will determine what size computer and what type of memory a business needs.

Paragraph 10

As computers develop, new words and concepts develop to explain them. Many of these terms take the forms of acronyms and initials such as RAM and CRT. Other words are formed by analogies to existing words and concepts such as *readout* and *software*. Nouns are sometimes converted to verbs and the appropriate verb endings are added, for example, *access, accessed, accessing*. The computer field changes very fast. A system developed three years ago may already be obsolete. Business persons who deal with computers must constantly update the information needed for this field.

Vocabulary Building Introduction

A: Vocabulary in context

Read the following sentences carefully and study the meanings of the italicized words or letters which are defined by the context.

1. Computers are high speed electronic machines which *process* data. Data in the form of a number is fed into the computer. The Universal Product Code (*UPC*) number is an example of data.

2. Data is *entered* by means of a *keyboard*, or it is *input* using a laser beam and optical character recognition (*OCR*). Banks use magnetic ink character recognition (*MICR*) to read data on checks.

3. The data is processed according to the *instructions* on the *program*. Computations are made according to *programmed* instructions.

4. The point of sale (*POS*) computer terminal has been programmed to match the UPC number with the name of the product and its current price.

5. A POS terminal is a *smart* or *intelligent* terminal which processes data and *displays* and prints out the *information*.

6. Input and output (*I/O*) terminals are *peripherals*. Input terminals are where the data is fed into the computer. Output terminals display or *print out* information resulting from the processing of the data.

7. The data is *displayed* on a cathode ray tube (*CRT*), which is like a television (TV) picture tube, or by a light emitting diode (*LED*) readout.

8. The output *information* from the POS *minicomputer* becomes input data which is fed into the larger central computer.

9. Computer equipment is referred to as *hardware*. Computer programs are referred to as *software*. Computer vocabulary is often formed by *analogy*.

10. An analogy is a correspondence or *association* between two dissimilar things. Hardware *corresponds* to the equipment. Since the opposite of hard is soft, the word *software* was chosen to refer to the *programs* for the operation of the equipment.

11. *Interface* devices, e.g., telephone cables, connect computers to their hardware. Hardware which is not part of the central processing unit (*CPU*) is known as peripheral equipment. *I/O hardware* and interface devices are examples of peripheral equipment.

12. A *binary* number system has only the symbols 0 and 1. A *binary* digit is a 0 or a 1. Binary digit is contracted to *bit*.

13. A series of eight *binary digits* can be used to indicate all the letters of the alphabet and all the numbers from 0 to 9. Such a series of eight *bits* is called a *byte*.

14. Computer *terminology* is often formed from acronyms. *Acronyms* are formed by using the first letter or letters of a *series* of words to form a new word. *Laser* is an acronym of *L*ight *A*mplification by *S*timulated *E*mission of *R*adiation.

15. Initials are the first letters of words. CRT, UPC, and LED are *initials*. When these initials form a word which can be pronounced, the word is an acronym.

16. Sales managers use the results they get from computers to help them plan ways to increase sales. Sales managers use *computer generated information* to develop marketing *strategies*.

Vocabulary Building

B: Matching

(Note: Due to the large number of computer terms, there are two vocabulary matching exercises in this lesson.)

Match the terms in the left column with the best explanations in the right column.

1. smart or intelligent ⎯⎯⎯ a . corresponding ideas, etc.

2. data ⎯⎯⎯ b . put into the computer

3. computer generated ⎯⎯⎯ c . unit of memory

4. strategy ⎯⎯⎯ d . produced by a computer

5. binary ⎯⎯⎯ e . method of reading bank check numbers

6. digit ⎯⎯⎯ f . display of lighted numbers

7. byte ⎯⎯⎯ g . plan

8. I/O hardware ⎯⎯⎯ h . refers to a terminal which processes data

9. CPU ⎯⎯⎯ i . having two parts

10. association ⎯⎯⎯ j . 3, for example

11. analogy ⎯⎯⎯ k . facts or numbers fed into a computer

12. software ⎯⎯⎯ l . computer terminals

13. LED readout ⎯⎯⎯ m. the part of the computer which does the computing

14. fed ⎯⎯⎯ n . programs

15. MICR ⎯⎯⎯ o . similarity or correspondence between two sets of things

C: Matching

Match the terms in the left column with the best explanations in the right column.

1. information ⎯⎯⎯ a . I/O equipment and interface

2. terminology ⎯⎯⎯ b . the first letter of a name

3. initial ⎯⎯⎯ c . method of reading UPC

4. laser ⎯⎯⎯ d . paper with *information* on it

5. series ⎯⎯⎯ e . a number indicating the name and size of a grocery item

6. printout ⎯⎯⎯ f . an ordered grouping

7. bit ⎯⎯⎯ g . TV picture tube

8. interface _____ h . an example of an acronym

9. corresponds _____ i . technical words

10. minicomputer _____ j . POS terminal

11. displayed _____ k . is matched

12. CRT _____ l . a 1 or a 0

13. OCR _____ m. computer output

14. peripherals _____ n . hardware for connecting computers to each other

15. UPC _____ o . shown on a screen or an LED

D: Multiple choice

The following exercise is designed to increase vocabulary and reading comprehension. Select the answer that best completes the meaning of the sentence.

1. Computers can be used to coordinate materials movement.
   a. The amount of materials to be used can be determined by the production schedule.
   b. Unused materials are not suitable for the computer.
   c. The program for materials movement is unrelated to the rate of production.
   d. Materials are input and manufactured products are output.

2. Managers make some decisions based on the information the computers provide them.
   a. The computer decides which course the company should take.
   b. A marketing decision might be based on population statistics.
   c. The data can tell them if they are making the correct decision.
   d. None of these.

3. Computers process data quicker than any human could.
   a. Because of computers many skilled workers have been replaced.
   b. Computers make many activities and analyses possible which could never have been performed before.
   c. Computers are not at all like other machines used in production.
   d. All of these.

4. There are three steps which describe the operation of the computer.
   a. Input/Output/Peripherals
   b. Punch in/Software/Hardware
   c. Input/Process/Output
   d. Feed in/compute/peripheral

5. Data is made up of various facts or concepts and it may be entered in several different ways.

   a. In the grocery store the UPC number is data which is entered by OCR.
   b. In a program designed for banking, the amount of a check and the account number are printed on the check with magnetic ink.
   c. The data and destination are punched into an airline ticket reservation computer.
   d. All of these.

6. The output of a computer is referred to as information. It is either displayed or printed out.

   a. It must also be entered as data.
   b. Bank statements, airplane tickets, and receipts are print-out information.
   c. This information can be displayed using OCR.
   d. The output appears on the interface.

7. A POS minicomputer uses a small laser beam to read the UPC.

   a. The laser is an example of peripheral hardware.
   b. This computer is also known as a smart terminal.
   c. This POS terminal displays the data and information on an LED display and sends it to a larger computer used for inventory control.
   d. All of these.

8. The computer field is divided into hardware and software.

   a. Only one of them is necessary for operation.
   b. The hardware is generally harder to operate than the software.
   c. Software refers to the program for using the hardware, or computer equipment.
   d. All of these.

9. Modern digital computers employ a binary number system.

   a. Because they are digital, they use all the numbers from 1 to 9.
   b. The two symbols in the binary system are 0 and 1. These binary digits are referred to as bits.
   c. The byte is the unit of memory referring to either a 0 or a 1.
   d. A bit often consists of eight bytes.

10. Computer terminology is formed using acronyms, initials, and analogies.

   a. All these terminologies are referred to as peripherals.
   b. Examples of these are laser, LED, and software.
   c. It's important to read out all software carefully.
   d. After these terms are learned, the student has mastered computer terminology.

Listening and Note-Taking Skills

E: Comprehension questions

Listen to the passage and answer the following questions about Paragraphs 1–6.

1. How are computers useful for production activities?
2. In what way are computers used in marketing and distribution?
3. How do managers use computer generated information?
4. What is electronic data processing?
5. In what way are computers like other business machines?
6. What are the three steps describing the operation of the computer?
7. What does the UPC number on a grocery item indicate?
8. What word describes the facts entered into the computer?
9. What word describes the output of the computer?
10. What is an example of output printed on paper?
11. Why is the POS terminal referred to as *smart* or *intelligent*?
12. Name two functions the POS terminal has been programmed to do.

F: Outlining

Write an outline beginning with Paragraph 1 and using the following headings.

I. Uses for Computers in Business
II. Comparisons (A. With other machines, B. With workers)
III. Three Steps of Operations
IV. The Operation of the POS Terminal

Reading Comprehension

G: Working with generalizations and examples

The text of this lesson first describes computers in general terms, and then follows this with examples. For instance, Paragraphs 1 and 2 discuss computer applications for business in general, and cite several examples of their use. In the following sentences you are asked to give examples for generalizations and make generalizations from examples.

1. Coordinating machine usage and materials movement is an example of computers used in which aspect of business?

2. In general, how are machines used in business and how is the use of the computer similar to the use of other machines?

3. What are two examples of the way data can be entered?

4. Give an example from the text of processing done by a program designed for banking.

5. In what ways can data be seen (visually displayed)?

6. What kind of peripheral equipment is used to read the UPC number?

7. What are examples of processing done by the POS computer?

8. Give an example from the text of information becoming data.

9. What kinds of I/O equipment would be used by an airline for a ticket reservation program? Explain the use of each.

10. What do we call a number system with only two digits?

11. The word *bit* is an example of what kind of word formation?

12. Give an example of a computer term formed by analogy and explain the analogy.

13. What is meant by the size of a computer?

14. Explain an *acronym* and give an example.

15. Name and describe one type of memory system.

Writing

H: Explaining through analogy

An analogy is a useful process of thinking. It can help a person understand new concepts in terms of already known concepts. There must be some apparent similarities between two concepts. From these similarities other similarities are inferred. For example, sometimes the structure of the atom is explained as being analogous to the solar system. The sun is analogous to the nucleus of the atom, and the planets are analogous to the electrons. Sometimes scientists refer to the orbits of the electrons. In other cases the electron may be analogous to a wave, while the wave motion of sound and light can be understood if an analogy is made with the waves of water.

An analogy can be drawn between the operation of the computer and the manufacturing process. For example, the input can be considered as raw materials. Write a composition in the form of an analogy explaining data processing as analogous to manufacturing. The general outline of the composition should follow the IPO sequence.

Vocabulary Review: Rephrasing

I: Rephrasing words and expressions

Rewrite the following sentences. Replace the words and expressions *in italics* with expressions from the text which have the same meaning.

1. One of the new *uses* for computers is in the development of marketing *plans.*
2. First the *facts or concepts* are *put into* the computer.
3. The data is *combined, sorted,* or *acted upon* according to programmed instructions.
4. The processed data is *shown* on a *television screen.*
5. The basic *order of events* for computers is *IPO.*
6. All products at the grocery store *bear a number which indicates the item and its size.*
7. *One type of peripheral device* is attached to a *cash register.*
8. This *minicomputer, which can process data and print out information,* is attached to a larger central computer for the entire store.
9. The printer prints *the name of the product* and the price on the *piece of paper given to* the customer.
10. Modern computers use a number system *consisting of only two symbols.*
11. Eight *binary digits* make up one *unit of memory.*
12. Two main divisions of the computer field are the *equipment* and the *programs.*
13. The *size* of the computer is determined by the number of *memory units* it can store on the memory chip.
14. Each byte can be *accessed* in the same amount of time regardless of *its position* using a RAM.
15. Some terms are just the *first letters* of the words which make up the term. Sometimes the letters form a word that can be pronounced.

Oral Practice

Debate

Resolved: All students should be taught the basic principles and terminology of computers. If they are to find jobs in the modern world, some understanding of computer operations is absolutely necessary—even if requiring this subject means dropping another subject. (Discuss the arguments for and against this.)

Glossary for Lesson Eleven
Computers

Access: the ability to communicate with the computer memory.

This terminal gives the operator *access* to the data.

(Also used as a verb.) The operator can *access* this information using this terminal.

Acronym: a word formed by using the first letter or letters of a phrase.

Laser is an *acronym* for Light Amplification by Stimulated Emission of Radiation. *Acronyms* are used to reduce long phrases to single words.

Analogy: a correspondence or relationship between pairs of things which is used as a basis for understanding or creating new concepts.

Since the word *hard* is the opposite of *soft*, by *analogy* the word *hardware* is a contrast with the word *software*. Hardware is the equipment. It is complemented by software, which is the program for using the equipment.

Application: in this lesson it refers to the use of the computer.

The computer has several *applications*. It can be used to record sales, control inventory, and keep business records.

Binary: refers to a system consisting of two elements.

A *binary* number system consists of the symbols *0* and *1*. *0* corresponds to an electric circuit being off and *1* corresponds to the circuit being on.

Bit: a contraction of the term *binary digit*.

The *bit* refers to one element of the circuit on a silicon chip. A system of eight *bits* can be used to represent all the letters of the alphabet and all the numbers from 0 to 9.

Byte: one unit of memory on a silicon chip; usually composed of eight bits.

The size of a computer indicates the number of *bytes*, or the amount of data which the storage device is capable of containing.

Capacity: refers to the number of bytes on which data can be stored at any one time, also the size.

The 128k RAM *capacity* of this computer is twice that of the smaller 64k RAM.

Cathode ray tube (CRT): an electronic vacuum tube in which a beam of electrons is projected onto a fluorescent surface which emits light.

Cathode Ray Tubes are used for television picture tubes. The output of the computer can be displayed on a *CRT*.

Central processing unit (CPU): the main part of a computer system where data is processed.

The *CPU* in this firm is too small for the amount of data to be processed.

Chip: a piece of silicon or another semiconductor which contains the memory circuits of a computer.

The *chip* used in this computer has a capacity of 64k bytes, but we are developing new *chips* which will have capabilities of 128k, 256k, and 512k bytes.

Code: a system of numbers, letters, or other symbols such as bars used to represent names, words, or items. (Also a verb.)

Most grocery products are *coded* with a number which indicates the item and its size.

Combine: to add to, join to, or mix with.

In the computer, data is *combined* with other data and instructions from the program as it is processed.

Computation: a mathematical operation.

The program for the POS terminal contains instructions for the *computation* of the sales tax.

Computer: an electronic machine for the processing of data.

The introduction of the *computer* has changed accounting procedures.

Coordinate: to control the actions and operations of more than one procedure so that they operate together.

Computers can be used to *coordinate* production volume with sales volume.

Data: facts and/or figures which will be entered into the computer for processing.

(Singular is sometimes *datum*). The amount of a check and the checking account number are *data* which the computer at the bank will process according to the instructions on the program.

Destination: the ultimate or final point of travel.

Computers used by travel agencies are programmed to print the flight number, the *destination*, the date and time, and the price on the airline ticket.

Electronic data processing (EDP): refers to the use of computers.

Electronic Data Processing has revolutionized the banking business.

Enter: to put data into the computer.

After *entering* the date, you should *enter* the amount of the check.

Generated: produced by the computer.

Managers base many of their decisions on computer *generated* information.

Hardware: here refers to computer equipment.

Input/Output *hardware* consists of keyboards and CRT terminals.

Information: output, processed data.

Information concerning the sale is printed on the customer receipt and used as data by the central computer.

Input: refers to the entering of data and the data which is entered into the computer for processing; (used as a verb and noun).

The first step in the use of the computer is *input.*

The data must be *input* before it can be processed.

Input-process-output, IPO sequence: the order or sequence of events in the use of a computer.

The operation of most computers follows the basic *IPO* sequence.

Intelligent or **smart:** a computer terminal which is able to process data and display or print out information.

The newest types of cash registers in stores are examples of *smart* terminals.

Itemized: refers to a list or display of individual transactions or items which gives details about each transaction or item.

The new cash registers print out *itemized* receipts which show the name of each product purchased and its cost.

Interface: a boundary or connection between two pieces of hardware, also the hardware that connects two pieces of equipment.

Several POS terminals are connected to the central computer by means of an *interface.*

Keyboard: a systematic arrangement of keys or switches which are operated by the fingers.

The arrangement of the *keyboard* for computer input terminals is the same as the arrangement of the keys on a typewriter.

Laser: an acronym for Light Amplification by Stimulated Emission of Radiation; a device for producing light waves of uniform wave length and phase which can be used to read optical characters.

The UPC numbers on grocery items are encoded by means of a series of bars which can be read by a scanner containing a *laser* beam.

Light emitting diode (LED): an electronic device which produces light when a small electric current passes through it.

The output can be read on the *LED* display.

Liquid crystal display (LCD): a crystal containing a liquid which changes color as an electric current is passed through it.

Like LED's, *LCD's* can be arranged to indicate numbers. *LCD's* require less current than LED's.

Magnetic: refers to the property of certain metals to attract iron.

Magnetic tape is used to record music, television, and electronic data. Bank checks are encoded with *magnetic* ink which can be read by bank computers. Banks use MICR (*magnetic* ink character recognition) to speed the processing of checks.

Memory: the ability of a computer to store data and information on a silicon chip.

The *memory* of this computer will be erased if the electric power fails.

Optical character recognition (OCR): the process of reading numbers encoded by a series of lines with a laser.

The UPC numbers on grocery items are entered into the computer by *OCR* as the item slides across the scanner.

Output: the information which comes out of a computer (also a verb).

The display of processed data is referred to as *output*.

Peripheral: refers to all computer equipment separate from the Central Processing Unit.

All I/O terminals and storage devices such as tapes and disks are called *peripheral* equipment or peripherals.

Point of sale (POS): refers to computer terminals connected to cash registers.

The use of UPC's depends upon the supermarket's possession of *POS* minicomputers.

Process: refers to the computations made by the computer (here, a verb).

After the data is *processed*, the information will be displayed on a CRT.

RAM (Random Access Memory): type of temporary memory system in which each unit of memory may be accessed in the same length of time regardless of its position on the storage medium.

Random Access Memory is one of the two basic types of semiconductor memories.

Readout: any kind of display on which the input data or output information can be read.

The total amount of the sale is displayed on an **LED** *readout*.

Reservation: here, refers to a specially designated seating space on an airplane, boat, bus, or train.

This computer program has been designed to process airline ticket *reservations*.

Scanner: a device which moves through a sequence of numbers or positions.

The UPC *scanner* uses a laser beam to read the bars that indicate the code number of a product.

Sorted: divided or classified into designated groups.

During processing the data is *sorted* according to the program.

Strategy: plan

Marketing managers use computers to develop marketing *strategies*.

Tape: the paper printout of a cash register; a device on which data can be stored away from the main computer.

The cash register *tape* contains information about the transaction. The profits for the last five years are stored on *tape*. Magnetic *tape* is coated with a magnetic sensitive substance and can be reused for the storage of data and information.

Terminal: the point or peripheral equipment where data is entered into or fed out of a computer.

The information will be displayed on a CRT *terminal*.

Terminology: vocabulary words specific to a certain field.

This lesson teaches you some basic computer *terminology*.

Universal product code (UPC): a system of numbering groceries and other items in which the UPC number, which is bar coded, indicates the name and the size of the item.

The *UPC* enables grocery store operators to use POS computers.

Worker hour, worker year: the amount of work which a worker can do in an hour or a year.

The computer performs a computation in minutes which would require hundreds of *worker hours*.

Answers

Lesson One:

A. Vocabulary in context

1. include
2. examples of
3. can provide
4. relate to
5. forms of
6. such as
7. activity of

B. Matching

a.	15	f.	3	k.	12
b.	5	g.	8	l.	13
c.	1	h.	2	m.	9
d.	6	i.	10	n.	4
e.	7	j.	11	o.	14

C. Completion

1. d
2. b
3. c
4. b
5. b
6. b
7. c
8. c
9. c
10. d

D. Noting details

Examples of production	Examples of financing	Examples of services
1. making airplanes	1. lending money	1. accounting
2. building buildings	2. trading stocks and bonds	2. distributing
3. constructing paper boxes	3. selling insurance policies	3. repair

E. Outlining

II. Four Factors of Business
  A. Land
    1. Real Estate
    2. Raw Materials
      a. on the earth's surface
      b. under the earth's surface
      c. in the air
  B. Labor
    1. Mental Work
    2. Physical Work
  C. Capital
    1. Wealth or Money
    2. Equipment
      a. tools
      b. machines
      c. buildings
  D. Entrepreneurship

F. Comprehension questions

1. by bringing together land, labor, and capital.
2. by deciding general policies for business operation.
3. four: initiation, management, innovations, and risk bearing.
4. what risk bearing involves.

G. Anticipating information

1. who the many people are.
2. what the biggest risk is.
3. If he is unskillful and unlucky, what will happen?

H. Rephrasing expressions

1. shares in the risks   3. Employees/work
2. goes bankrupt   4. entrepreneur
            5. creditors

Lesson Two:

A. Word analysis

1. organization, obligation, corporation   4. ability, continuity
2. ownership, proprietorship, partnership   5. requirement
3. disposition   6. difference

B. Vocabulary fill-ins

1. decide   5. bankrupt
2. owner   6. continue/satisfaction
3. decision/equipment   7. equip
4. differ   8. satisfy/continue

D. Matching

a. 10   e. 9   i. 4
b. 3   f. 7   j. 1
c. 5   g. 2   k. 12
d. 6   h. 8   l. 11

E. Multiple choice

1. d   6. b
2. a   7. c
3. a   8. b
4. c   9. b
5. b   10. a

F. Outlining

A. Definition: Business with Single Owner
B. Starting the Sole Proprietorship

    1. purchase goods, equipment
    2. set up shop
    3. few government regulations

C. Operating the Business
   1. owner makes decision
   2. takes risks
   3. no tax on business

D. The Successful Business
   1. owner pays tax on profits
   2. takes personal satisfaction

E. The Unsuccessful Business
   1. business closes
   2. owner sells inventory and equipment
   3. pays bills

G. Organizing information into categories

Advantages	*Disadvantages*
1. opportunity for success	1. risk of ruin
2. owns all assets	2. supplies all capital
3. makes decisions	3. takes responsibility for errors
4. keeps all profits	4. owes all debts

H. Analyzing a paragraph

1. Sole proprietorship
2. Partnership
3. Corporation

I. Outlining by noticing parallelism

4. Partnerships

   A. Definition—Business with More than One Owner

   B. Starting the Partnership
      1. assets contributed by each partner
      2. how partnerships can be changed or terminated

   C. Operating the Business
      1. partners' own assets
      2. debts owed
      3. make decisions based on expertise of each partner
      4. no tax on business—personal tax on share of profits

5. Advantages and Disadvantages
   A. More Capital Available
      1. unlimited financial liability
      2. agreement necessary on policies
   B. Two or More Managers

J. Comprehension questions

1. The corporation is very *different* from both, so it will not.
2. Yes, because personal ownership in sole proprietorship and partnership are both unlimited liability and profits are distributed to owners, while in a corporation there is limited liability and profits go to the shareholders.
3. It sells stock.
4. They are taxed, retained, paid as dividends and taxed again.
5. He sells his shares.
6. Liability is limited to assets.
7. It must have good organization for its many managers.

K. Rephrasing words

1. single owner/enterprise
2. begin/end
3. chance/runs the risk
4. wealth/settle/case
5. partners/debts/share
6. raise capital/wealth
7. bankruptcy/liability
8. retains/reinvest in the company
9. share owners/dividends
10. monitored, regulated

Lesson Three:

A. Parts of speech

1. continuous
2. assembly/assembling
3. standard/standardization
4. extraction
5. productive
6. synthetic
7. analysis
8. manufactured
9. process
10. specified/specifications

C. Topic sentences

Production means making something of value/Production creates wealth.

D. Outlining

II. Types of Production

    A. Analysis
        1. definition: separating into several parts
        2. example: oil

    B. Synthesis
        1. putting together
        2. glass

    C. Extraction
        1. mining
        2. petroleum

    D. Fabrication
        1. assembly
        2. automobiles

E. Organizing information into categories

Intermittent	*Continuous*
1. short production runs	1. long production runs
2. low volume	2. high volume
3. custom made	3. standard goods
4. adjustable machines	4. specialized machinery
5. flexibility	5. standardization
6. increased labor	6. less labor
7. expensive	7. less cost per unit

F. Multiple choice

1. b		6. c
2. a		7. a
3. b		8. a
4. b		9. b
5. a		10. a

H. Rephrasing words

1. extract
2. volume
3. consumer
4. efficient
5. manufacturer's specifications
6. analyzing/individual
7. fabrication
8. customer
9. custom made
10. job lot

Lesson Four:

B. Matching

a. 4   f . 11   k . 2
b. 5   g. 12   l . 15
c. 9   h. 13   m. 1
d. 10   i . 14   n . 7
e. 6   j . 3   o . 8

C. Completion

1. duplication   6. interchangeable
2. idle   7. uniform
3. inventory(ies)   8. adapted
4. shutdown   9. retool
5. unit cost   10. morale

D. Outlining

I. Introduction

    A. Definition: Arrangement of Workplace, Equipment, etc.

    B. Reasons for:
       1. smooth operation
       2. elimination of bottlenecks
       3. minimum buildup of inventories
       4. increased productivity
          a. reducing walking distances
          b. keeping supervisors close to job

II. Planning

    A. Considerations
       1. workers
       2. type of work
       3. method of production
       4. cost

    B. Reasons for:
       1. plant, buildings cost a lot
       2. efficient use reduces costs

    C. Method
       1. design layout
       2. design building to suit

E. Comprehension questions

1. continuous and intermittent
2. product
3. petroleum, automobiles
4. process
5. furniture

F. Multiple choice

1. b
2. b
3. a
4. c
5. b
6. a
7. c

G. Understanding main ideas

1. Advantages of product layout
2. Efficient use of machinery; inventory control
3. By controlling and coordinating the use of machines
4. They can be stacked, palletized, loaded, and shipped
5. Control and supervision are simplified

H. Methods of development

1. Disadvantages of product layout.
2. No.
3. 1) breakdown means total shutdown; 2) specialized machinery is not adaptable; 3) changes can usually be made only once a year; 4) inflexible rate of production; 5) lack of employee morale.

I. Outlining

4. Product layout: definition
5. Advantages of product layout
6. Disadvantages of product layout
7. Functional layout: definition
8. Advantages of process layout
9. Disadvantages of process layout

L. Rephrasing words and expressions

1. planned/arranged/move/least confusion
2. for smooth operation, for the elimination of bottlenecks/for minimum buildup
3. there is a favorable working environment

4. helps to increase worker productivity/keeping costs down.
5. is based on
6. set up to suit a particular
7. unit cost
8. consumed/fixed rates
9. there is a breakdown at any point/shutdown
10. they can be easily palletized

Lesson Five:

B. Matching

a. 7   e. 8
b. 6   f. 4
c. 2   g. 1
d. 5   h. 3

C. Parts of speech and vocabulary fill-ins

1. authority/authorized
2. apply/application/applicants
3. promotional/promoted
4. description/describes
5. base
6. competing
7. determination
8. required/requirements
9. qualified/qualified
10. recruitment

D. Outlining

II. Recruiting
   A. Reasons for:
      1. to replace workers who retire or quit
      2. to fill new jobs created by expansion
   B. Management—Determines Goals of Company and Positions Needed
   C. Personnel Department—Finds Qualified People
   D. Internal—Person Selected from among Current Employees
      1. Promotion
         a. more authority and responsibility
         b. increase in salary
      2. Transfer
         a. from one department to another
         b. different working conditions or hours

3. Result of internal promotion policy
   a. managers worked their way up
   b. new employees hired at starting positions

III. External—Persons from Outside the Firm
   A. From College Campuses
   B. From Competitors
   C. From Advertisements and Placement Services

E. Listing specific information from a narrative

1. basic information about the company
2. title of the position
3. duties/responsibilities
4. where position fits on organizational chart
5. qualifications
6. salary and fringe benefits
7. how to apply

F. Completion

1. b	6. b
2. c	7. d
3. d	8. d
4. c	9. d
5. a	10. c

G. Comprehension questions

1. testing, assigning points for experience and education.
2. personality of applicant and ability to work with others.
3. A prospective employee is an applicant for a job.
4. development of personnel policies.
5. for fair and equal treatment of all employees. Decisions are made on a case by case basis resulting in poor morale.
6. paid vacation, sick leave, etc.—all things received in addition to pay.
7. An employee feels he has been treated unfairly.
8. to look after the interests of the workers.

I. Rephrasing words

1. staff	6. qualifications
2. recruit/retire	7. fringe benefits
3. a competitor	8. applicants
4. grievances	9. recruits externally
5. promotion	10. transferred

Lesson Six:

A. Rephrasing ideas

1. Paragraph 1, sentence 2
2. Paragraph 1, sentence 4
3. Paragraph 1, sentence 5
4. Paragraph 2, sentence 1
5. Paragraph 2, sentence 3
6. Paragraph 2, sentence 4
7. Paragraph 2, sentence 5
8. Paragraph 2, sentence 6
9. Paragraph 3, sentence 1
10. Paragraph 3, sentence 2

B. Matching

a. 10
b. 4
c. 7
d. 9
e. 2
f. 1
g. 5
h. 8
i. 6
j. 3

C. Form and content clues

arr = arrangement of ideas; m = meaning of ideas.

Paragraph 1

several - arr
refers to - m
other - arr
related to - m
another - arr
indicates - m
when - arr
mean - m
determine - m
such as - m
and - arr
includes - m

Paragraph 2

in the past - arr
emphasized - m
task of - m
accomplished by - m
included - m
in addition - arr
involved - m
consists of - m
such as - m
and - m

Paragraph 3

encompasses - m
but - arr
different - m
notion that - m
in other words - m
therefore - arr

Paragraph 4

now - arr
involves - m
first - arr
solely - arr
on the other hand - arr
thus - arr

D. Comprehension questions

1. a. stock market   b. grocery market   c. supply and demand
2. It includes many meanings.
3. sales promotion, distribution
4. advertising, personal selling
5. a. transportation   b. storing   c. related services
6. a. financing   b. standardization and grading   c. risk bearing
7. Para. 2 in the past . . . selling
   Para. 3 the *modern* marketing . . . general
8. Past: product first, sell later; Now: see if it will sell first, then produce it.
9. desire of consumers becomes a factor.
10. Production is an engineering problem; marketing involves considering human behavior.

F. Analytic questions

1. distribution
2. place utility adds value
3. a) large quantities;   b) no special treatment;   c) low cost.
4. raw materials such as raw rubber, crude oil, ores, coal.
5. Rail freight is less expensive than truck freight because special treatment probably costs more.
6. Trucks are faster than rail or ship.
7. Finished goods are more expensive. Customers require products faster. It's a service to the customer.
8. Finished products represent more value—the value of labor and raw material. Generally, inventories must be financed.
9. All factors and aspects must be considered together.

G. Multiple choice

1. c	6. b
2. b	7. b
3. b	8. b
4. c	9. a
5. d	10. d

I. Rephrasing words and expressions

1. determine, supply, demand, consumers.
2. emphasized sales.
3. task of figuring out
4. physical distribution
5. storage, financing, standardization and grading.
6. encompasses

7. subscribes to the notion, by consumption.
8. deciding, designing, satisfy.
9. separated
10. merchandise freight, smaller.

Lesson Seven:

A. Rephrasing ideas

1. paragraph 1, sentence 1
2. paragraph 2, sentence 1
3. paragraph 2, sentences 4, 5
4. paragraph 2, sentence 6; paragraph 3, sentence 1
5. paragraph 3, last sentence
6. paragraph 4, sentence 3
7. paragraph 4, sentence 6
8. paragraph 6, sentence 2
9. paragraph 6, sentence 3
10. paragraph 7, sentence 2
11. paragraph 7, sentence 4
12. paragraph 8, sentence 2
13. paragraph 8, sentence 3
14. paragraph 8, sentence 12
15. paragraph 8, sentence 14.

B. Matching

a. 14
b. 5
c. 6
d. 1
e. 15
f. 9
g. 10
h. 12
i. 8
j. 7
k. 4
l. 2
m. 13
n. 11
o. 16
p. 3

C. Completion

1. c
2. a
3. c
4. b
5. d
6. b
7. c
8. d
9. d
10. b

D. Vocabulary in context

1. person who purchases something for his own use.
2. producer
3. simplest form of distribution.
4. people who take possession of merchandise and take title to it or arrange for transfer of ownership.
5. ownership
6. consumer; one who desires and buys a product.

7. one who actually takes title to the merchandise.
8. one who arranges for the transfer of title between manufacturer and wholesaler.
9. products having a low price, and can be found at several convenient locations.
10. the closest places.

E. Comprehension questions

1. the producer
2. middlemen
3. they collect the various products and give them place utility.
4. the manufacturers
5. he divides them into amounts and customers.
6. he transports them to where they are needed, required.
7. agent, merchant
8. broker
9. type of product
10. convenience

F. Outlining

I. Middleman

    A. Job of the middleman
      1. collect
      2. divide
      3. deliver

    B. Types of middlemen
      1. Merchant middleman; example of activities:
        a. owns warehouse
        b. buys quantities
        c. distributes
      2. Agent middleman; puts buyer and seller together

II. Convenience Goods

    A. Definitions, examples: low price, gum, cigarettes, etc.

    B. Customer considerations: convenience

    C. Location of sale, examples: supermarkets, convenience stores, machines

    D. Method of distribution: side, several middlemen

III. Shopping Goods

    A. Definition: cost more

    B. Customer considerations: price, quality

IV. Location of Sale

    A. Full service retail store
        1. personnel: salespeople
        2. product: on display
        3. cost: of space and commission added to product

    B. Discount store
        1. personnel: small sales staff
        2. product: merchandise that moves, smaller selection
        3. cost of space: lower, discounts from manufacturers

    C. Franchise stores — Chain stores
        1. similarities
            a. merchandise
            b. operation
        2. differences
            a. independently owned
            b. owned by parent company
        3. advantages
            a. distribution
            b. vertical integration
        4. disadvantages
            a. efficiency sometimes lost
            b. sometimes large expensive bureaucracy

G. Comprehension questions

1. The route the product takes from manufacturer to ultimate consumer.
2. A person who arranges for transfer of merchandise from producer to consumer through distribution system.
3. Because products needed by one company or consumer are produced at scattered locations.
4. 1) collect products 2) divide into amounts needed by consumer 3) transport
5. He takes title to merchandise.
6. He arranges for transfer of title.
7. convenience
8. wide distribution
9. inexpensive products purchased frequently without much thought.
10. 1) price 2) quality
11. salespeople, demonstration of product.
12. same merchandise, same name
13. license to operate a business under a certain name.
14. franchise—independently owned; chain—owned by parent company.
15. owns all aspects of business from production to final sale.

16. advertising, distribution, name recognition
17. Large company that owns smaller companies or branches of a chain.
18. promotion, distribution, supplies
19. better cost control, higher profits
20. an organization too large to be efficient; bureaucracy.

I. Rephrasing words and sentences

1. trade channel; products
2. middlemen; ultimate consumer
3. office purchasing agent; that is convenient
4. distribute/transport; warehouse; retail stores
5. broker; commission
6. transfer of title
7. is on display
8. features; demonstrates its use
9. overhead costs
10. appliances
11. are vertically integrated
12. inflexibility
13. maximize profits
14. a franchise

Lesson Eight:

B. Matching

a. 5	f. 22	k. 14	o. 8	s. 11
b. 19	g. 16	l. 6	p. 12	t. 9
c. 20	h. 17	m. 4	q. 1	u. 7
d. 21	i. 10	n. 18	r. 13	v. 15
e. 2	j. 3			

C. Multiple choice

1. a	6. b	11. b
2. c	7. d	12. d
3. a	8. d	13. d
4. b	9. a	14. d
5. b	10. b	15. d

D. Vocabulary in context

1. *shift the demand curve*: change graph to show increased desire of consumers for product.
2. *keep sales constant*: sell the same amount of the product or service.
3. *elastic demand*: consumer desire for product changes under certain conditions.

4. *sales volume*: amount of product or service sold.
5. *offset*: make up for, balance, compensate for.
6. *promotion*: attempts to influence customer to purchase product.
7. *presentation*: method of distributing information.
8. *aimed at*: intended for, given to, told to.
9. *media*: methods of presenting information, method of communication.
10. *wide audience*: a large group of listeners, viewers, or readers.
11. *justify*: to make the effort worthwhile.
12. *demand*: desire of customers for goods or services.

E. Comprehension questions

1. advertising
2. mass audience
3. nature of product, distribution of market, type of information to be conveyed
4. TV
5. cost of production justified only by numerous showings
6. newspapers
7. salespeople, sales representatives
8. many examples possible
9. commission
10. demonstrates product, negotiates price, designates specifications of product

F. Outlining

I. Advertising

A. Definition: non-personal presentation of goods, services, or ideas aimed at a mass audience.

B. Choosing a method — depends on product, distribution of market, type of information to be conveyed.

C. Media
   1. television
      a. sight and sound
      b. high cost of production
      c. repetition to justify cost
   2. newspaper
      a. time-specific
      b. geographically specific

D. Best working situations
   1. when demand increases
   2. when there is a noticeable difference between products

E. Purpose: to communicate information which will convince customer to purchase.

II. Personal Selling

    A. Definition: sales person trying to convince customer personally.

    B. Effectiveness

        1. concentrated market

        2. industrial goods

        3. high unit value of product

    C. Activities of Salesperson

        1. sell exactly what customer needs

        2. demonstrate product

        3. negotiate price or terms

III. Sales Promotion

    A. Need for in self-service environment

    B. Basic types

        1. Information

            a. pamphlet/booklet

            b. demonstration

            c. market research

            d. dealer training

        2. Stimulation

            a. free samples

            b. reduced price

            c. premiums

            d. coupons

    C. Other: displays

G. Comprehension questions

1. The sales personnel can deal directly with potential customers and not waste time and energy trying to deal with a mass of non-customers.

2. There is not a mass market for industrial goods. The market is concentrated.

3. The salesperson can demonstrate the use of the product, and the cost of the product would justify paying the salesperson a commission.

4. To negotiate about the trade-in allowance and the price.

5. Sales promotion involves several activities, and it is important where there is no sales staff.

6. A demonstration. A salesperson deals with the customer, explaining the features of the product.

7. They stimulate customers to buy.

8. A premium is an extra item granted the customer free with a purchase. A coupon is a certificate that grants a discount.

9. By making them easy to see and reach.
10. New customers; the competition's customers.
11. Spread information to new potential customers or new geographical areas.
12. Remind the customers of the name of the product; compare the product with others.
13. Providing marketing information; seeking shelf and display space.
14. Contests, coupons, price discounting.
15. The company must design a total program of promotion for a particular product.

I. Rephrasing expressions

1. supply; demand
2. demand curve
3. should be inelastic
4. sales volume; offset
5. convince
6. suitable; widely distributed
7. convey; regarding
8. television advertising is; a mass audience
9. media
10. can appear on a particular date; distributed to particular geographic areas
11. emphasize; the competition
12. the market is concentrated
13. the general public
14. justifies paying; fee
15. individually tailored
16. the salesperson; negotiation
17. a trade-in
18. demonstrate the product to the customer
19. market research
20. premium
21. of the display
22. coupon
23. retailers; carry
24. to increase market share; shelf space
25. stimulate/convince

Lesson Nine:

B. Matching

a. 20	f. 13	k. 19	p. 9
b. 16	g. 3	l. 2	q. 15
c. 7	h. 18	m. 5	r. 12
d. 14	i. 4	n. 17	s. 10
e. 1	j. 6	o. 8	t. 11

C. Multiple choice

1. c	4. b	7. c
2. b	5. a	8. d
3. c	6. c	9. c
		10. c

D. Comprehension questions

1. to find out if they are making money.
2. journal
3. book of original entry
4. sales, uses of raw materials, purchases
5. posting
6. all the accounts
7. account
8. accounting
9. construct financial statements
10. basis for business decisions
11. financial condition on a specific date
12. both sides are equal
13. left side
14. net worth
15. current, fixed
16. cash or items to be turned into cash in the current business period.

E. Outlining

I. Financial Records — to find out if company is making a profit.
   A. Journal — to record daily business transactions
      1. examples: sales
      2. uses of raw materials
      3. purchases
   B. Ledger — posting
      1. definition of account: financial record of similar transactions
      2. examples
         a. sales account
         b. costs of raw materials

II. Bookkeeping
   A. Used by small business owners to determine profits/losses and taxes.
   B. Used by accountants to construct financial statements.

III. Balance Sheet
   A. Definition: financial statement indicating condition of a company at a certain time.
   B. Description: left side itemizes assets, right side itemizes liabilities and equity.

IV. Current Assets
   A. Definition: cash or items to be turned into cash in current year.
   B. Examples
      1. merchandise
      2. receivables

F. Completing an outline

    V. Fixed Assets

        A. Definition: those kept and used for a long time.

        B. Examples
          1. machinery
          2. production equipment

        C. Value Less Depreciation
          1. Definition: cost minus decline in value due to use and wear
          2. Example: taxicab cost $12,000; used for 3 years; subtract $4,000 each year.

    VI. Other Fixed Assets

        A. Furniture

        B. Fixtures

        C. Buildings

        D. Land

    VII. Liabilities

        A. Current: paid during current business cycle
          1. accounts payable
          2. taxes payable

        B. Long term: paid in ten, twenty, or thirty years (with interest added)
          1. bonds
          2. mortgages

    VIII. Owners' Equity

        A. Corporation: value divided by number of shares' book value.

        B. Sole Proprietorship/Partnership: value of business to owners.

G. Comprehension questions

1. It is turned into cash that same year.
2. They can readily be turned into cash.
3. A bad effect. Merchandise is not converted to cash at the expected rate.
4. fixed asset. Cost less accumulated depreciation.
5. divide cost by years of useful life.
6. affect method of calculating depreciation.
7. building shows depreciation.
8. current assets/fixed assets; current liabilities/long-term liabilities.
9. long-term liabilities

10. current liabilities
11. with a mortgage property is secured. A bond is based on the reputation of the company.
12. both long-term liabilities.
13. assets minus liabilities.
14. net worth divided by shares of stock.
15. The company could be purchased for less than its net worth.

I. Rephrasing words and expressions

1. maintain financial records; making a profit
2. journal
3. transfer figures from the journal into
4. information in accounts; financial statements
5. as a basis for; income tax liability
6. assets; liabilities; owner's equity
7. balance sheet; liabilities; owner's equity
8. current assets; fixed assets
9. merchandise; money owed the company
10. liquidate
11. depreciation
12. depreciation schedule; part of
13. fixtures; depreciation
14. liabilities
15. guaranteed by the value of
16. bonds; reputation

Lesson Ten:

B. Matching

a. 21	g. 20	m. 10	s . 17
b. 18	h. 2	n . 4	t . 19
c. 22	i. 6	o . 8	u. 11
d. 5	j. 12	p. 16	v. 13
e. 1	k. 14	q. 7	w. 23
f. 3	l. 9	r . 15	x . 24

C. Rephrasing ideas

1. c	6. c
2. d	7. a
3. b	8. d
4. d	9. d
5. d	10. b

D. Comprehension questions

1. develop economies, increase production, meet market demands.
2. countries exchange goods which they produce efficiently.
3. It affects agricultural production.
4. They produce labor intensive products.
5. Countries produce goods that afford them a comparative advantage.
6. Countries exchange goods which they produce more efficiently for goods other countries produce more efficiently.
7. They can accumulate wealth.
8. subsidies, tax benefits.
9. to protect domestic industry.
10. labor unions.

E. Completing an outline

I. Advantages of World Trade

   A. development of economies

   B. increased production

   C. increased business opportunities

II. Production Efficiency and World Trade

   A. efficiency results from
      1. climate
      2. raw materials
      3. labor force
      4. geographical location

III. Two Theories Regarding International Trade

   A. Adam Smith's Theory — absolute advantage. Trade develops when countries produce what they produce most efficiently.

   B. David Ricardo's Theory — comparative advantage. Trade develops when countries produce certain goods more efficiently than trading partner.

IV. Government Policies

   A. Encouragement of exports: country becomes wealthier
      1. market information
      2. trade mission
      3. subsidies
      4. tax incentives

   B. Control of imports
      1. taxes
      2. quotas

V. International Monetary Exchange
   A. Exchange rates: floating rates determined by supply and demand of currencies.
   B. Balance of payments
      1. surplus — country exports more than it imports.
      2. deficit — country imports more than it exports.
VI. Multinational companies
   A. Creation — company sets up production facilities in several countries
   B. Methods of operation — based on comparative advantage of countries where they operate.

F. Comprehension questions

1. It provides economic development.
2. transportation, marketing, distributing.
3. 1) labor pool;   2) climate;   3) natural resources;   4) location.
4. Absolute advantage of Smith vs. comparative advantage of Ricardo.
5. They receive money for selling exports.
6. It would damage local industry.
7. to provide jobs, to control the market for that product.
8. quotas and tariffs.
9. Tariffs raise revenue.
10. Tariffs increase cost, quotas restrict supply.
11. Value would tend to increase.
12. The currency would become weaker because more of it would be flooding foreign markets.
13. to save transportation costs.
14. A large company that owns smaller companies.
15. 1) to develop its economy;   2) to provide employment for its population;   3) to lower balance of trade deficit.

H. Rephrasing words and expressions

1. realize the advantage of
2. unskilled workers; are labor intensive
3. theorized; free market
4. there would be an international division of labor
5. export; domestically
6. control
7. subsidize
8. domestic
9. restrict; levying; duty
10. a tariff; revenue
11. legal tender
12. exchanged
13. fluctuate; supply and demand
14. has a balance of trade surplus
15. parent; subsidiary
16. global

Lesson Eleven:

B. Matching

a . 11
b . 14
c . 7
d . 3
e . 15
f . 13
g . 4
h . 1
i . 5
j . 6
k . 2
l . 8
m. 9
n . 12
o . 10

C. Matching

a . 14
b . 3
c . 13
d . 6
e . 15
f . 5
g . 12
h . 4
i . 2
j . 10
k . 9
l . 7
m. 1
n . 8
o . 11

D. Multiple choice

1. a
2. b
3. b
4. c
5. d
6. b
7. d
8. c
9. b
10. b

E. Comprehension questions

1. They coordinate materials movement, machine usage, and work schedules.
2. for processing sales orders, arranging delivery schedules, and keeping track of shipments.
3. for accounting: as a basis for a decision.
4. The use of computers to process data.
5. They perform time-consuming routines and repetitive work.
6. Input; Process; Output.
7. The name of the product and size.
8. Data.
9. Information.
10. Receipts, bank statements, airline tickets.
11. It processes and prints out information.
12. It computes tax, prints out names of items and prices, the total purchases, records sales, and computes change.

F. Outlining

I. Computers in Business

    A. Production, Planning, and Coordination
        1. materials movement
        2. machine usage
        3. work schedule

    B. Marketing and Distribution
        1. develop strategies
        2. process sales orders
        3. arrange delivery schedules
        4. keep track of shipments in route

II. Comparisons

    A. Perform Boring and Routine Work Like Other Machines

    B. Perform Work Much Faster than Human Counterparts

III. Three Steps of Operation

    A. Input
        1. entry of data
          a. keyboard
          b. magnetic tape
          c. newer methods
        2. types of data: various facts and concepts
          a. amount of money
          b. travel destination

    B. Process: Data Combined, Sorted, or Acted Upon
        1. bank balance adjusted to deposits and withdrawals
        2. ticket price to destination
        3. grocery price to item

    C. Output: Called Information, Displayed in Several Forms
        1. on CRT
        2. as digits
        3. printed on paper

G. Working with generalizations and examples

1. production
2. to do tedious, routine, and difficult jobs.
3. OCR scanner, punched in, MICR
4. Subtracting checks from account balance; producing bank statements.
5. LED; CRT; LCD
6. LASER
7. Computing totals, recording sales.
8. UPC—POS computer—Information—central inventory output of POS becomes input for central computer control.
9. keyboard to punch-in destination. CRT to see schedule of routes. Ticket printer to print out ticket.
10. Binary
11. Contraction
12. Software opposite of hardware; soft opposite of hard.
13. the number of bytes it can store.
14. Using initials to form a word: RAM, LASER.
15. RAM: Random Access Memory—any byte can be accessed at the same speed.

I. Rephrasing words and expressions

1. applications; strategies
2. data; entered
3. processed
4. displayed; CRT
5. sequence; input, process, output
6. have a UPC number
7. An OCR device; POS mini computer
8. 'smart' or 'intelligent' terminal
9. the item purchased; receipt
10. binary number system
11. bits; byte
12. hardware; software
13. capacity; bytes
14. read or changed; where it is stored
15. initials; an acronym

Skills Index

The pages specifically indicated are where the individual skills are first introduced or emphasized. Most of the skills listed, however, appear on other pages as well.

Content skills in specific business areas

Linguistic/structural skills

Listening/speaking skills

Debating, 12
Interviewing for a job, 81
Listening for clues, 9
Noticing details, 9
Note-taking and outlining, 9, 10

Organizational skills

Classifying and categorizing printed information, 26
Developing ideas logically in writing, 59
Developing short and extended arguments orally, 12
Understanding and dealing with oral argument by others, 12

Reading comprehension skills

Analyzing, 26
Anticipating information, 11
Classifying and categorizing, 26
Comparing and contrasting, 24
Completing sentences, 7
Drawing conclusions, 91
Drawing inferences, 110
Identifying main ideas, 57
Making generalizations, 11
Making judgments, 78, 92
Reading for details, 11
Sequencing, 91, 92

Vocabulary development

Analyzing words and their derivations, 22
Matching words with descriptive phrases, 6, 7
Rephrasing expressions and ideas, 11, 12, 89
Using context clues to understand new words, 5, 6

Writing skills

Analyzing and summarizing, 58
Composing a job description, 78
Contrasting ideas, 41, 42
Developing a scenario of related events, 171
Filling out a job application, 71
Outlining, 10
Practicing informational paragraphs, 12
Using analogy and parallelism, 26
Writing informational compositions, 59
Writing topic sentences and developing them, 28